AMBOS NOGALES

The publication of this book was made possible in part
by a grant from the Ethel-Jane Westfield Bunting Foundation
and the National University of Ireland.

AMBOS NOGALES
INTIMATE PORTRAITS OF THE U.S.–MEXICO BORDER

Photographs — **MAEVE HICKEY**
Text — **LAWRENCE TAYLOR**

School of American Research Press
Santa Fe

To the people of Nogales and in memory of Ben Taylor.

School of American Research Press
Post Office Box 2188
Santa Fe, New Mexico 87504–2188

Acting Director: Cynthia Welch
Editor: Jane Kepp
Designer and typographer: Katrina Lasko
Printed and bound by C & C Offset Printing Co., China

Library of Congress Cataloguing-in-Publication Data:
Hickey, Maeve. Ambos Nogales: Intimate Portraits of the U.S.–Mexico Border
photographs, Maeve Hickey; text, Lawrence Taylor.
p.   cm.
ISBN 1-930618-07-7 (pbk.:alk. paper)
1. Nogales (Ariz.) Social life and customs—Pictorial works.
2. Nogales (Nogales, Mexico)—Social life and customs—Pictorial works.
3. Nogales (Ariz.)—Social conditions—Pictorial works.
4. Nogales (Nogales, Mexico)—Social conditions—Pictorial works.
5. Mexican–American Border Region—Pictorial works.
6. Mexican Americans—Arizona—Nogales Region—Pictorial works.
7. Immigrants—Arizona—Nogales Region—Pictorial works. I. Taylor, Lawrence J. II. Title.
F819.N63 H53 2002
972'.17—dc21   2002017659

Library of Congress Catalog Card Number 2002017659
International Standard Book Number 1-930618-07-7
First edition 2002.

■ CONTENTS

■ PREFACE

AMBOS NOGALES IS THE THIRD BOOK WE HAVE DONE TOGETHER—all of them explorations in photographs and words of the borderlands of Arizona and Sonora. One book led to another, and all of them led to the two Nogaleses, nonidentical "twin" towns joined and divided by the border.

We began working in the region in 1994, exploring the old and new Nogales Highways. The resulting book, *The Road to Mexico*, offers two parallel journeys, one in photographs and the other in words, that take the viewer/reader through a series of encounters with the landscapes, artifacts, and, above all, people of that dynamic and often surprising borderland. Appropriately, *ambos Nogales*—"both Nogaleses"—occupy the center of that book, for there we discovered that the shape assumed by the ambiguous border depends largely on with whom one crosses it.

One group of habitual border-crossers new to the frontier were the members of a gang called El Barrio Libre, who became the subject of our next book, *Tunnel Kids*. These refugees from broken and impoverished families in various parts of Mexico had found a niche for themselves in the cavernous drainage tunnels that emptied floodwaters from Nogales, Mexico, into Nogales, Arizona. In those subterranean passages they guided, then often robbed, undocumented immigrants. Called rats and vampires, they were, we found, entirely human, children forced by circumstances well beyond their control to find ways to survive in what for them was a frightening but also alluring space. Together, they acted out their fragile collective identity—in which the irony of their self-described "free barrio" did not escape them—and managed to form, if only for extended moments, the families they desperately needed. In all that, they seemed to embody the tragedy and creativity of the border, and with their cooperation and collaboration over a series of summers (1995–98), we put together a book that tells their stories and presents them through a series of portrait photographs.

1

The tunnel kids appear again in this book, but in more candid photos and in a few vignettes offered as parts of the larger composite picture of the two border towns. That composite picture is conjured through images both quiet and exuberant (the photos and scenes described are again from the period 1995–98)—images of what for us is a dramatic and endlessly surprising revelation of the human spirit. We hope here to evoke and suggest through fragments, visions, and encounters a world in which human life is, paradoxically, at its most constrained and most liberated.

In the course of this project we benefited from the generosity and support of many people and organizations in three countries. We owe everything, of course, to very many of the people of *ambos Nogales*. On the Sonoran side, we would like to particularly mention the students and staff of CECADEE technical school, Ramona Encinas, the López family of Colonia Solidaridad, the clients of Mi Nueva Casa, Loida Molina, Gilbert Rosas, and especially Alberto Comacho. Across "the line," we thank the staff of the Americana Motor Hotel, the staff of the Paul Bond Boot Company, Judy and Roger Borey of the Boys and Girls Club, Sheriff Tony Estrada, the officers of the Nogales Police Department, Yvette Gonzalez Serino and Connie Serino, Judge Jan Smith Flórez, Liz and George Thomson, the United States Border Patrol (particularly Rob Daniels of the Tucson sector and officer John S.), and Pam and Teddy Wingfield. Very special thanks go to Claudia and Mati Proto.

Farther afield, we are grateful for opportunities given us by the Department of Anthropology at the University of Arizona to discuss and present our work and receive valuable comments, suggestions, and help in many forms, particularly from Melissa McCormick. We were also helped by El Rio Community Center, Douglas Foley and Debbie Byrd, and Gregory McNamee. We thank Jane Kepp, Katrina Lasko, Nancy Owen Lewis, Elizabeth McCann, Joan O'Donnell, Douglas Schwartz, Cynthia Welch, and all the staff of the School of American Research, especially Jeanne Fitzsimmons. Also in Santa Fe we thank James Dunlap and Barbara Sommer of Allá bookstore and gallery, as well as Martha Sandweiss and Robert Horowitz. And as always, our warmest appreciation goes to Lisa Otey and Kathleen Williamson in Tucson.

In Ireland, we have been aided in numerous ways, and we are particularly grateful for the always generous support of His Excellency Daniel Dultzin, Ambassador of Mexico in Ireland. Also at the Mexican Embassy we thank Miguel Angel Vilchis, Head of Missions, and the entire staff. We are grateful as well to Ambassador and Mrs. Michael Sullivan of the United States Embassy in Ireland, Dr. Patrick Wallace, Director of the National Museum of Ireland, Professor John Kinsella of N.U.I. Maynooth, and Bruce Swansey of Trinity College. Thanks to the students and staff of the Anthropology Department at the National University of Ireland at Maynooth, especially Deirdre Dunne, Yvonne Leckey, and Lynne Wyse. For their advice and assistance, we are grateful to the

Gallery of Photography, Dublin, and especially its director, Tanya Kiang, as well as Pete Smyth and the staff. The publication of this book was supported by a grant from the National University of Ireland, for which we are very grateful.

Our warmest appreciation must go to family, especially Mr. and Mrs. Philip A. Hickey. Thanks as well to Tommy Hansen in Rhode Island and to Janice Taylor, Peter Weinstein, and Harriet and Ben Taylor in New York. As always, to Daria, for everything.

We gratefully acknowledge funding from the Arizona Humanities Council, the National University of Ireland, and the School of American Research through the Ethel-Jane Westfield Bunting Foundation.

4

MEMO'S NEIGHBORHOOD

La ciudad se ilumina para nuevas proezas
The lights of the city come on for further exploits
—Homero Aridjes

"NOGALES—NO ES MÉXICO, ES UNA CARICATURA DE MÉXICO," Señora Valdez spat in disgust as we rattled and bumped through the swirling chaos of Avenida Obregón. She was there visiting her grown son, Roberto, who had been living in Nogales, Sonora, for most of his life. Roberto had always gone to visit his mother's place amid the rural splendor of Michoacan, so it was more than thirty years since the señora had visited Nogales. Coming from her country home on a lake in that southern part of Mexico, she was shocked by the filth, racket, and confusion.

"I remember a different place," she said. "Sure, there were tourist shops, but it was still a Mexican town, with a central plaza. And people would dress up to come to the square on Saturday night." She paused, looking forlornly out the car window.

"Life there had a beauty and a rhythm. But now . . ." Her voice trailed off in dismay as she looked east at the fragments of what had been the *zócolo*—the central square in and around which Mexican town life is always lived. There were only the shattered remains left by the new, wider road, now always choked with traffic heading for the great arcing cement structure that guarded the U.S. border. The townspeople she had known were gone, replaced by hordes of day-tripping tourists and a sea of the waiting, hustling, or celebrating poor.

"I'll tell you what this town has become," she said, still scowling. "This morning I go to see my friend Ana—who has the perfume shop near the hotel. A man, a beggar, is out in the street asking for money 'para comer'—to eat. Inside, Ana is enjoying a big breakfast in the back. I say to her, 'Come on, you've plenty.' So we fix a beautiful plate of eggs and beans and tortillas for the poor man, and I hand it to him like he is a guest at a very nice hotel. What does he do? He holds it up to his nose, sniffs, and then hands it back to me, shaking his head with disdain! Ana nearly fell down laughing."

So did we, but the señora was still not amused.

5

"Look," Roberto said, "that is the way we are here—everybody has a right to his own craziness. Like the guy who walks on Obregón all day with only one shoe on. The cops think he may be scaring the tourists—like they aren't going to buy pots if they see something so strange. So yesterday one of those new tourism cops goes up to him and says, 'Hey, you've only got one shoe on!' So he looks down and then back at the cop and says, 'Hey, I always wear only one shoe!' The cops didn't know what to say, but I said to them, 'Puro Nogales.' And they had to laugh, man."

I was laughing, too, but I understood the señora's perspective. She had arrived on a bus from the south the night before and had taken a cab to one of the few decent hotels in the city center. We had picked her up there and had been forced by one-way roads to drive almost into the United States before circling back. Now, our route up Obregón was the way all visitors from the North first see Nogales. Like the main drags of all the bigger Mexican border towns, that avenida runs perpendicular to "the line," leading the tourist south into a Mexico that presents itself as colorful souvenir shops and cantinas.

"Sí, una caricatura!" Roberto repeated his mother's remark with amusement.

We parked on one of the side streets, leaving Señora Valdez to make her way to her hotel. She already needed a siesta. Maeve and I followed Roberto to see his pal Memo, who ran one of the smaller tourist shops—barely more than a cluttered alcove just off Obregón. As always, Roberto was carrying his guitar, Nina, not only because he liked to be ready for music at all times and places but also because he couldn't risk leaving his only remaining valuable possession in an apartment that was burgled every week or two. He was hoping for a duet with his friend. But Memo had taken the day off, as we heard from his young assistant, who was busy trying to coax Americans into the shop with the standard patter—a rhythmic, memorized hawker's English: "In here folks! Don't you want some more Mexican junk to bring home?"

He turned then to Roberto and switched to Spanish. "Memo? He had a late night. You'll find him at home, sleeping it off."

"Well, it's nearly noon, so let's go wake him!" Roberto said, clutching Nina like a weapon.

We followed him on foot through the crowds around the border gate—tourists and locals streaming past women selling homemade tortillas, and the usual row of Indian women and children arrayed on blankets piled with the cheapest sorts of curios.

"You want a mask or, for only a few pesos, a tiny, head-bobbing wooden turtle?"

Roberto paused to eye one of the women from a safe distance. Though dark, she had neither the hairstyle nor the dress of an Indian. "My ex-girlfriend," Roberto mumbled, "a photographer—selling fucking wooden turtles on the street. We had a big fight and she left. I think she's seeing someone else."

We continued up Avenida Ingenieros, which runs parallel to Obregón, just to the west of it, but reveals a different Nogales. It climbs and doglegs along its broken path through the old quarter of the city, past soft pastel adobe homes and small neighborhood shops. We turned west through a clutch of young kids playing soccer in the street and then mounted a cobblestoned road so steep that it soon gave way to stairs winding ever higher among terraced yards and tile-roofed *casitas*.

The last house at the top of the hill was Memo's: a long, low adobe of the style called "territorial" in Arizona. It was surrounded by blossoming shrubs, and a pillared *portal* in front afforded a shaded view out over the city, which seemed to lie miles below us. We had grown used to the unrelenting din and were now stunned by the serene quiet, broken only by the sporadic mumbling voices of women from within the house. Roberto called out a greeting, and two women appeared—Memo's sister and niece.

"He's sleeping!" his sister informed us, chuckling. "After the night he had! You want him? You can't raise the dead!"

But Roberto had already taken out Nina, and to the amusement of the whole household—all of them were soon out on the *portal*—he began to strum and sing, looking up in the direction of Memo's window. It was a sonorous love song, a serenade begging a reluctant lover to rise from her bed. Whether it was the music or the accompanying laughter, Roberto's persistence was eventually reward-ed and the screen door banged open.

Memo did not seem pleased. He stood there, shirtless and shoeless, red eyes glowering at us from beneath a tousled mop of hair. But Roberto sweetened the tune, and Memo could not keep himself from laughing. He went back inside and reemerged with cans of beer for everyone, and a few minutes later a revived, if still shaky, Memo offered to lead us through his neighborhood: a hilltop, cobble-stoned, secret corner of the city.

To one side of his house an alleyway twisted past tiny vacant lots and then into a narrowing maze between adobe walls. It seemed a peaceful dream of old Mexico—though the graffiti hinted of another side of local life. One name, El Negro, appeared frequently, and then I heard it spoken: "Negro, cómo estás?" It was Memo, greeting a short, dark, surly young man leaning against a shaded wall, smoking. He was one of the leaders of a local gang—Los Rolling Stones—Memo told us after we had gone on, though it was hard to picture the flyweight sleepy figure in so active a role. Except, that is, for the stitched-up eye.

The next lane was so narrow that we found ourselves nearly scraping the screen doors of homes, within which we could see families preparing their midday dinners. The air was heavy with the heady aroma of lard and beans. One of the doors banged open as we passed, and a large black dog skidded into the alley, barking and nipping at Maeve's heels.

8

We emerged eventually into an open square, awash in the white glare of the afternoon. Around us stood what seemed a quiet village set deep in the heart of Mexico. A whir of fans and tinkle of dishes were barely audible outside the thick-walled adobe row houses that closed off every view. Among them were a church and, most enigmatically, a life-size dummy dangling from the top of an electric pole. The slim figures of children darted in and out of the shadows, leaving one home and disappearing into another. Then, suddenly, we heard music, the familiar strains of the local radio station, La Poderosa—the Powerful One—booming from an old car parked in the center of the square. A few children were busy washing it, and they paused to grin at the strangers when they saw our interest.

Leaving Maeve to photograph the kids and the square, Roberto, Memo, and I entered what I thought was an abandoned shack, until I saw it boasted a sign: La Pasadita. Inside, a tiny old woman was barely visible behind a wooden counter. Around her were narrow shelves filled with examples of every one of the thousands of snacks and sweets that Mexico produced, arranged like precious, brightly colored gems in a treasure chest. Memo crawled up on a chair there, as if the sweet shop were a bar, and bought us all *paletas*—frozen fruit bars—against the sweltering afternoon. "Sí, hay mucho calor!"— it is very hot—the old lady remarked, leaning back against the wall and surveying her immaculate little kingdom with the pride it deserved. We sat quietly within, nursing the *paletas* and looking out into the still sleepy afternoon.

"It's quiet now, all right," Memo said, no doubt reading my thoughts. "But at night, it's a different matter. Fights, drugs—the lot. You don't wander through these streets at night."

Nevertheless, I did find myself back in the neighborhood that very night, after an evening with Roberto and Memo spent visiting a series of border bars along Canal Street, by the border fence. One, El Sonorial, was bright pink inside, every barstool home to a two-hundred-pound prostitute, each tightly wrapped in a black six-inch miniskirt or a spandex cocktail dress, feet jammed into impossibly small, pointy high heels, which they were busy swapping—giggling like teenagers–with one another. We joined them, sipping Pacíficos and watching a scene that would have delighted Toulouse-Lautrec —a splendid, if sometimes frightening, carnival of characters: laughing dwarfs, swaggering drug lords, silver-toothed lesbian whores. And all to the lively music of a bass-spinning *grupo norteño* followed by an incredibly loud silver-buttoned Sinaloa brass band. The most startling thing was my own reflection—the entranced if bewildered gringo—which caught my eye in the mirror behind the bar as I followed one scene after another.

Then it was next door to a larger but less lively bar for billiards and male bonding. We made our winding way out into the still-pulsing midnight streets and stopped at the *depósito* for half a dozen *cahuamas*—liter bottles—of Tecate. Finally, it was slowly up the roads and stairways to Memo's.

9

This time we went behind the house, where I could see that it had been built into the steep hill-side, leaving the roof only a few feet above the ground in the back—a perfect roost for making music and enjoying the blessedly cool night air.

Memo's drunken, aging hippy brother, Jorge, was there waiting for us, happy for the arrival of *cahuamas* and the promise of entertainment. "You're American," he noted. "Did you ever see Jim Morrison?" He went on in that vein, remembering dead rock musicians, while Roberto and Memo picked their guitars, struggling to find one another and make music. Somehow, they could not quite manage. I thought that they were simply too drunk, but Roberto later told me that he was out of joint because he had seen his ex-girlfriend again that afternoon, with her new guy.

They gave up finally, and we all stretched out on the clay roof, admiring the giant mountain laurel that had grown its way through the concrete yard above and behind us. It was exploding with flowers, and the aroma overwhelmed the beer. A thousand blossoms shimmered in the black night.

I turned to look out over the city below us, spread out under a continuous blanket of stars. To the south, the sea of flickering little lights lit miles of colonias—the shack slums, now home to nearly three hundred thousand Nogalenses, that circled and greatly extended the periphery of the old city. As in so many of the Mexican border towns, most of these people were recent arrivals from the south. They were seeking work in the nearly one hundred foreign-owned assembly plants—*maquiladoras*—or else they hoped to cross the border.

That dream was also clearly visible from Memo's roof. Almost below us, the border fence was interrupted by the huge cement archway of the gate, where drivers, even this late at night, were still coming through and being stopped and asked to explain who they were and where they had been or where they were going. Beyond the customs complex was the town of Nogales, Arizona, where the far fewer lights lay in more orderly rows under towering signs for McDonald's and Burger King. There, too, the old town hugged the border—two parallel shopping streets where Mexicans came in decreasing numbers to spend their devalued pesos on Barbie dolls or Rolexes. Beyond that were a few blocks of old houses, and then the broad and empty new highways lined with widely separated shopping malls. With something like a tenth the population of its so-called twin, it was no wonder that the American Nogales seemed small and sparse, its line of highway lights disappearing into an endless, night-black desert.

12

14

■ LAS PLAZAS

El día se va despacio,
La tarde colgada a un hombro,
Dando una larga torera
The day goes slowly,
Afternoon swung from a shoulder,
Sweeping a bullfighter's cape

—Federico García Lorca

¡CORRIDA DE TOROS!

Posters all over both Nogaleses announced the bullfights next Sunday in the Plaza de Toros "La Macarena," promising the confrontation of "four brave bulls from the famed Trincheras" with the "young rivals from Tijuana, 'The Reckless' Paco Aviña and the valiant and artistic José Rodríguez 'Joselin.'"

We had been eager to revisit the *plaza de toros* of Nogales, Sonora. Although it was neither an ancient Roman coliseum—like the buildings that sometimes serve that function in Europe—nor an elaborate modern construction, the old arena had a grandeur appropriate to the small city, with dramatic frescoes above the gates and living passion within. Some tourists, but more often relatives from north of the border, would join the local populace there on a Sunday afternoon for the endlessly reenacted story of death without resurrection. For whatever one may think of the treatment of the bulls, the cruelty—if that is the right word—comes from intimacy rather than distance. In killing the bulls, the performers confront their own—our own—mortality. The Spanish, and the Mexicans, believe in death. They do not yet share the American fantasy that it can be overcome with proper diet and exercise. And the dance of life and death is heightened and mirrored by that of male and female. As flows the blood of death, so too fall the red roses on the same sand, offerings to matadors of sequined, graceful, almost delicately powerful masculinity from striking beauties in white lace blouses and flat black hats.

The plaza was there where it had always been, but it seemed, even from a distance, changed. The paint around the bullfight frescoes was peeling away, leaving gray concrete patches, and the base of the arena was pocked with holes.

"There are no more bullfights here," said a man wandering by, as though I had asked. "They made a new plaza on the edge of town. Here, there is nothing."

18

But that was not true either.

So we discovered while walking around the arena. I spied a man sitting out on a ledge—the top of the first tier of the arena wall. But then he disappeared, like a snail into his shell, sliding backward and dropping into a hole behind him. I looked inside. He had withdrawn further, but a cardboard sleeping pad and a pile of soiled clothing showed that this was home. Hearing a shout, we peered through an eyehole in the wall a few yards farther along. Inside, the gray gloom was penetrated by a few columns of sunlight that had found their way through holes in the roof. Suddenly, two little boys leaped into view, squealing with delight. Now, the whole arena seemed to vibrate into life before our eyes. Like the Roman coliseums after the fall of the empire, this plaza was another site of decay and repopulation. Squatters had found every niche and cavity; each single man or little family had captured and defended a tiny space, a concrete cave. The old city had reached a kind of Dark Age, and the arena was now a warren of the dispossessed.

Their debris lay everywhere. Off to one side, where rocky, weedy ground rose behind the arena, a trash heap was strewn with broken glass and empty spray paint cans—the drugs of the street kids. In the small crevasses hollowed between wall and trees were the remnants of recent occupation: scraps of worn clothing, bottles, even reading matter in the form of comics.

We climbed the steep ground behind the building, leaning against the outer wall as our feet slipped in the loose, gravelly sand, reading the graffiti as we went. Mounting a rocky outcrop at the top, we were able to look over into the arena. Within was silence and dust—and where the charging bull should have been, an old station wagon was decaying slowly in the midday sun.

The bullfight was to take place in the new *plaza de toros*—La Macarena—on the southern edge of the city. We drove through six miles of cars streaming like cattle through the streets, only occasionally deflected in their path by big-bellied policemen in T-shirts and sunglasses. Just before the city gave way to desert, the very last roads led off to the west and east, all of them freshly plowed, wide dirt boulevards into either the newest colonias or the assembly plants—*las maquiladoras*.

On the corner of one of these roads was a tiny, handwritten sign with an arrow that pointed west toward the "Corrida de Toros." We turned, seeing only huge dirt hills pushed up to the north and south to make way for the road and a large field for parking.

I was already disappointed. From the outside, the new arena had all the majesty and romance of a low-budget Little League baseball field. Two sets of bleachers—simple, tiered, wooden benches—faced into a ring enclosed by wooden panels plastered with advertisements for businesses on both sides of the border. No sign advertised the traditional two-price division between a sunny and a shady side of the arena: *sol y sombra*. Not a sliver of shade was to be found anyway, either in the plaza or on the surrounding bare dirt hills, onto which a few families had dragged beach chairs for a free view of the proceedings. The whole dusty world was baking in the fierce July afternoon sun.

We nearly left, but eventually we decided to join the few dozen others foolish enough to pay ten dollars to die of boredom and heat prostration. Maeve went off with her cameras, and I sat and surveyed the crowd. Not many Mexicans, I thought. But we were there at the advertised hour, and after another forty-five minutes or so, the other patrons began to arrive. By the time an hour had passed, the place was filled with boisterous families, avid men with judging eyes, and even a few dark-eyed beauties.

Beyond the arena I could just make out the flash of sequins in the sun as the performers donned their costumes. But still we saw no sign of the bulls. I turned to a man sitting beside me and asked him if he knew the cause of the delay. "Customs," he said. "Two of the bulls are 'Americans,' and they are having some difficulty crossing them." He smiled at the obvious irony of border politics. And once again I realized how good Mexicans are at waiting. I have been in Mexican train stations when a delay of twelve hours was announced and everyone simply unrolled blankets on the floor and settled in for a sleep. Here, too, everyone was prepared to wait, not with a nap but with a song and a dance. The popular tune "La Macarena" blared over the loudspeaker—was that the source of the new plaza's name? —and dozens of spectators rose to their feet and did the hip-swaying movements that even Senator Al Gore had been seen to perform on American TV. At least the scene is lively, I thought, as this exercise was repeated half a dozen times or so over the next hour, until the truckloads of bulls rumbled through the parking gate, sending up clouds of desert dust.

Maeve was still roaming "backstage" among the performers and their retinues when the first event was announced by more canned music. Another bad sign, I thought, listening to a particularly tinny version of the standard *corrida* theme. The crowd seemed to be enjoying itself, but I remained unconvinced that this paltry new arena was going to prove a worthy replacement for the old one.

Within, the fighting dancers had taken their positions, and the first of four bulls, a Sonoran from "Trincheras," stormed into the arena. It was already furious, wildly charging every flick of the capes, spinning on a dime and stabbing the air as the toreadors hopped to the side. The matador walked slowly around the arena, his cape draped casually on his arm, watching the bull's performance, learning its moves, and preparing for the later confrontation. Next came the picador, who looked very young, a nervous boy furtively blessing himself as his mount high-stepped into the arena—his first *corrida*, the announcer informed us. Without hesitation, the bull charged him from the side and, hooking both horns under the horse's heavy cloth "armor," tried to flip the two-headed beast over. It nearly succeeded. The shocked rider, frantic to keep his seat in this his debut performance, clung desperately to his horse while toreadors waved their capes and finally drew the frenetic animal away. Determined to make up for his embarrassment, the young picador wheeled his horse—now snorting with confused fear—and drove his lance into the bull's meaty shoulder. Blood flowed freely from the wound, but the bull seemed neither weakened nor slowed, only angrier than before. Once more it managed a powerful assault on the horse and nearly threw picador and mount to the arena ground. Again, the toreadors drew the bull away, and again the boy pursued his foe, inflicting more wounds before trotting out of the arena to appreciative applause. He was followed by three men on foot, *banderilleras*, each armed with two ribboned, bladed sticks, who took turns running, sometimes pirouetting, up to the bull and planting their gaily colored weapons into its shoulders.

Finally, all was ready for the handsome young matador, Paco Aviña, "The Reckless," who danced the now bloody bull around the arena until he was ready for the well-named moment of truth. The sword penetrated perfectly, piercing the beast's heart. The bull stared blankly for a second and then collapsed, first to his knees, and then to his side. Paco cut off its ear and, holding the trophy high, did his slow walk through a shower of roses, cheered by the adoring crowd.

I watched the horsemen drag the poor bull from the arena by its tail and then wandered out to see the backstage area, easily accessible in this rudimentary plaza. The bustle and confusion was that of any stage between the acts of a play, opera, or ballet—with performers, costumes, and props all in motion—but with one other element. At the edge of the "dressing rooms" stood a shrine: a wooden stand with candles and a painting of the Virgin in one of her many aspects. She was La Macarena Esperanza—the Madonna of Hope—a very different source for the name than the popular dance tune. A strange combination, I thought, but how typical of a Mexico whose popular Catholicism seemed unaffected by any separation of sacred and secular—of the holy and the wildly playful. But of course moments of purity rose from within that apparent chaos, like the one I witnessed as the matador who was next to fight, "Joselin," knelt solemnly before the Macarena and prayed with fervor before blessing himself and rising to his fate.

He had reason to pray. Unlike Aviña, who enjoyed a reputation and a considerable following, Joselin was relatively unknown. The crowd seemed to reserve judgment as he made his first tentative approaches to his bull. His work, I thought, would not be easy. Although the bull had come through its bout with the picadors with a blood-streaked neck and chest, it seemed more resolute than tired. Whereas the first bull had thrown itself wildly at its adversaries, this one seemed to look and think, pawing the dirt in classic fashion and then charging with determination. In this dance, the bull led. Although the matador swirled his cape over the bull's back, he did it always with a slight step to the side, giving right of way to the rushing animal. The fight continued in this fashion, slow and undramatic, as the crowd waited restively for the kill.

Finally, the matador was ready. Choosing his moment, he approached the panting bull and, with the proper, graceful, arcing gesture, stabbed. Whether he was too tentative or simply miscalculated, the sword went no more than a few inches into the bull, who threw it across the arena with an angry toss of his head. The crowd was less patient than it might have been with a more popular matador and began to mutter. No doubt shaken by his misstep and anxious before a less than friendly audience, the young matador retrieved his weapon and, after a few more turns with the bull, tried again to take its life. And again failed. And then a third time. Each attempt missed its mark or lacked the force to find its way deep into the bull, and each time the bull shook the sword off like an annoying fly and continued to prance and snort around the arena. The crowd was now favoring the bull, and the poor matador was clearly desperate.

Then something happened. Joselin's face—till then bathed in sweat and twisted by shame— seemed for a moment transfixed as if by an apparition. Perhaps it was La Macarena he saw before him. He sheathed the sword in the cape and with incredible calm walked directly up to the bull, pushing the cape into the animal's startled face. The bull charged, but the matador simply turned on his feet, letting the animal fly by only inches from his beautifully arching body. The crowd—unsure—cheered softly. The matador walked away, his back to the bull, and then—as if it were the most casual of decisions—turned again toward his opponent. Once more he walked directly up to the bull and, flourishing the cape before its angry bobbing head, taunted the beast into furious but ineffective action.

Now the crowd was getting happier, and the matador saw no reason to hasten the moment of truth. Again and again he teased the bull into wild charges under his floating cape, never losing his ground or his serene expression. The bull was left standing, still angry but bewildered, in the center of the arena.

Now, I thought, the matador will try again to finish him off. But he had other plans. He walked calmly to within two feet of the bull and, holding the cape behind him, reached forward and placed a hand on the beast's black forehead. The crowd was entranced—it watched in happy shock. Could this be the same man who had so disappointed only moments before? The bull did not react, and the matador spun on his feet, flourishing his cape, and goaded it into a few more charges.

Now everyone was ready for a glorious end, but the matador seemed transported into another realm. Master of himself and of the bull, he found a fearless grace that could be expressed only through yet more daring intimacy with his thousand-pound foe. Once again he approached the bull, but this time he dropped to his knees and, looking down with the teasing eyes of a playful lover, held the cape out to the right. The bull charged, and the matador, without rising from his knees, lifted the cape and let him pass. The animal turned, but so did the man—still on his knees. And so the fight continued with several more passes until the bull finally swung its head too close and, catching Joselin's vest, threw him to the side like a bale of hay. The crowd was on its feet, but so was the matador—with some blood on his face, but with an unshaken resolve that led him back to the bull. Again on his knees, he reached forward and caressed his enemy between the horns. We were all standing in excitement, fear, and wonder as the matador finally rose to his feet and slowly turned in a circle to face every one of us. He then drew his saber from the cape and, wearing a mask of religious beauty, plunged the weapon deep into the bull's black body.

28

29

■ LAS COLONIAS

Oh ciudad de los gitanos!
¿Quién te vio y no te recuerda?
O city of the gypsies,
Who that has seen you can forget?
—Federico García Lorca

"¡NOGALES. NO ES UN RANCHO, ES UN CORRAL!"

That was Blanca's view of her city. It was the perspective of one of the "cattle."

We were sitting on a couple of battered, half-woven beach chairs in the dirt in front of her home in La Solidaridad. Around us was the most randomly formed and positioned array of houses imaginable. To one side was a tar-papered shack with one window and a draped-plastic doorway, and across the dirt path, a four-room brick house with neatly arched windows and a paneled wood door. Beyond were hill after sandy hill of plywood and cardboard hovels, cinder block shops and houses, and a sea of tin roofs glinting in the last rays of early evening.

Blanca's own home was a compromise between her dreams and what she could now afford. A poured concrete slab floor supported a house of cardboard.

"I arrived here two years ago, and it was crowded then, but it's worse every day!" she told me, craning a sun-lined neck to survey the surrounding scene.

If Nogales is a corral, I thought, then it has only one fence: the international border. No need for any barrier on the southern side, for few go back. They only keep coming up—wave after wave looking for something better than what they have.

"We came here like everybody else, looking for work—from the state of Jalisco, from a village near Guadalajara. My husband and I and three of the children. Since last year we have a fourth."

"Guadalajara is the home of mariachi!" I said, speaking of one of my favorite Mexican musical forms.

"Yes," she laughed, "in our *tierra* we had much music but little work. My husband is a welder and there was nothing for him there. So we came up here. But he doesn't find welding work here, and I am in the factories—the *maquiladoras*."

Like all the big border towns, Nogales had assembly plants—*maquiladoras*—that were paying between four and five hundred pesos a week—forty or fifty dollars. Impossibly little from the

American point of view, but something like twice as much as wages farther south—when work was to be found at all. So it was not hard to understand why the population had swelled over the last several decades, especially since the early nineties. Nobody knew how many people lived there, somewhere around three hundred thousand souls. Most of them found shelter in the great arc of colonias that ringed the old city up to the border on the east and the west, with beautiful and inviting names like Buenos Aires, Las Brisas, Los Tapiros, or Blanca's own Solidaridad.

"The jobs are not what we thought," Blanca explained. "The work is very, very boring. You put little pieces on bigger pieces, and you are always falling asleep. Why wouldn't you? You can't get enough sleep in a place like this, and then you have to get up very early to get to work. See, I must go down to the shop on the main road, and there I get a minibus that will take me to Obregón, and from there a regular bus to the industrial park. ¡Ay mami! That's a lot of time and trouble—and you must pay. So when I work at those places I must get up at maybe five o'clock. And so, as I said, you can easily fall asleep over the little pieces."

"But the money isn't bad?" I offered.

"Sure, it's not bad—but look at the expenses!" Blanca continued. "There are the buses, then the meals. Well, they give you breakfast when you get there—a little bit—but the dinner, in the middle of the day—that you pay for. It's deducted from your wages."

She paused and then looked around the neighborhood before continuing. "But the big problem is the money to be here—here on the border. Everything costs much more here. Food, clothing, everything. The land we are building on here costs one thousand dollars. That's right, this little piece of land. And the price stays in dollars, so if the peso falls—as it always does—it costs more. But what was our choice? I know a woman from work whose family bought in Colosio, do you know that place?"

In fact, I did. We had visited that most peripheral of colonias with a friend some weeks earlier. The full name was "Colonia Luis Donaldo Colosio," after the assassinated presidential candidate. The neighboring colonia, "Diana Laura Riojos Colosio," memorialized his wife. A Sonoran from nearby Magdalena de Kino, Colosio had been shot during his 1994 campaign, and his glamorous young wife had died of cancer only months later. An irresistibly tragic tale. We had visited their graves in Magdalena not long after their deaths and watched the streams of pilgrims, many of them starry-eyed adolescents who looked at the grave as if it were home to fallen rock stars. Since their demise, much had been named after the Colosios, not least in Nogales. The ring road that led around the city to the truck crossing was now El Periférico Luis Donaldo Colosio. And then these two colonias—or perhaps more accurately future colonias, at least in the latter case.

We had entered Colosio along a freshly plowed dirt road, quite near the new *plaza de toros*. The car nearly surfed on the loose yellow dust, rounding a corner and descending into a giant empty space backhoed out of the surrounding desert hills. Looking like a stage set, or the beginnings of one, for a comic frontier western, it comprised only a dozen or so homes and a shop—all of them built of wood scraps that must have been dumped off the back of a truck. We saw one modest concrete structure: a clinic purportedly open for a couple of hours a week. That's how colonias begin, I had thought, and just as I was wondering what basic services the residents had, a truck loaded with five-gallon clear plastic jugs of drinking water rumbled in.

"In places like that, you have even less than here," Blanca continued, "and you are farther from everything. So we put everything into this piece of land."

I surveyed their empire—a tiny sloped lot, mostly of bare sand strewn with rocks and weeds. Below us hundreds of red ants were streaming out of their nest, heading for our feet. One thousand dollars for this, I thought, and then remembered that the price of a coyote-guided passage to the United States was about the same, depending on one's final destination. These were the investment choices. The coyote was undoubtedly the higher risk, but the potential payoff here was certainly limited.

"What's it like to live here?" I asked.

"The hardest part is that you don't know people," Blanca answered as we dragged our chairs from the path of the ants. "My cousin Diana is just over there. She came here first and has built a brick house. But she is the only person I know. I will nod hello to a few others—the ones you see every day—but most people here [she swept an arm around] are strangers. Surrounded by strangers. That is very different from home. There we were poor, everyone was, but we were all neighbors, more or less. Here you don't know who to trust, so you trust no one."

"Here comes my cousin now," she observed, squinting in the failing light. A hefty woman in a long skirt was walking briskly toward us through a pack of children and animals, no doubt curious about me.

"How did the demonstration go?" Blanca asked her cousin, then turned to me to explain. "The city turned off our water—it's more than two weeks now!—and so Diana went with a big crowd to the water authority pump on Avenida Tecnológico to protest, to demand they turn the water back on. This is Lorenzo," she concluded, remembering to introduce me.

"Mucho gusto, Lorenzo," Diana greeted me, and then told the story of the meeting.

"Well, it's the fault of Wenseslao Cota Montoya. He was elected mayor on the PRI ticket and he came in promising us that he would solve all our problems and improve the distribution of drinking water. That was more than nine months ago. Not only isn't the situation better, it is worse! Two weeks ago they turned off the *tomatera del pozo*—that's the pipe that brings water to all the colonias on this side

of the city. And so finally we got organized. A number of people went around from house to house asking us to show up, and a few thousand did. The crap you hear from them though—the officials! The Sanitation Department said that tests showed the water was contaminated. A man from Colonia Tapiros said that his colonia has been getting water from that pipe for more than thirteen years without any word of contamination. Now, suddenly, it's not safe—and they claim this without showing us one word of proof!"

That is the way things work here, I thought. The government makes promises, supplies contaminated water, and then cuts it off, while the people of the colonia "manage" in their own fashion. I remembered reading a newspaper item in which an official explained that every time the water authority laid out a few hundred yards of pipe to a legitimate customer, many others tapped into it, creating an illicit network of pipes far more extensive than the official one.

"Did you get satisfaction?" I asked. "Will they turn it on?"

"The leader of the demonstration is meeting with the mayor tomorrow—so we'll see." Diana did not look hopeful.

I decided to check in on Blanca's husband, Felipe, the welder, who was banging away on the far side of the house.

"Hola, Lorenzo," he greeted me, lifting the plastic visor from his eyes. He was putting what looked like the finishing touches on a rolling metal street-vendor's cart.

"If I can't get a job welding, I can at least use my welding to make a job for myself," he laughed. "With this cart I will sell *exquisitos* in town." I was myself beginning to develop a taste for that borderland version of a hot dog, wrapped in bacon and drowned in chiles and salsa. I wished him luck in his enterprise. Felipe looked over at his house. I supposed he was thinking about what it would take to complete it, to make it a good place for his family. I asked him what plans he had. But he looked from his house to the surrounding neighborhood, as if he were taking stock of the larger enterprise.

"This is some place to live, Lorenzo," he said finally. "Did you hear what happened last week? Just down where the road crosses the railroad tracks?"

I had, in fact, for the story had been in all the newspapers—on both sides of the border.

"Two policeman—*municipales*—were gunned down. Executed with bullets in their heads. They were only boys themselves. And now they have arrested another cop—a Beta. He was the one who had found them and reported it, and now they say he is the one that shot them. Drugs."

An incredible tale, but hardly an isolated incident. There had been a murder every few days for the past two weeks, most of them looking like the assassinations typical of drug wars. The Mexican twist was that the police forces—which seemed to behave like the private armies of warlords—were clearly implicated in these struggles. In this case, Grupo Beta, an elite border force newly introduced with much publicity as "incorruptible," was believed to be at the center of things. And not only with the drug trade. That morning there had been another story in the papers reporting that Betas were often seen bicycling up to the notorious Hotel Miami, center of operations for the smuggling of illegal immigrants into the U.S., and collecting wads of dollars from the coyotes running that business.

Blanca had joined us during Felipe's tale of drugs and death. She added, "And there is the more usual crime of the streets here. Cholos everywhere, either breaking into your house or robbing you on the road. Just the other day, a young man from Las Brisas was walking home late at night. A gang of cholos surrounded him and gave him a beating. They took his wallet, of course, but they also took every stitch of clothing on him. He was left beaten and naked in the middle of the road."

Just then, Blanca and Felipe's sons, Miguel and Carlito, ran up from the road below, shouting greetings. I knew them from the streets and had not guessed that they had what appeared to be a fully functioning family.

"Lorenzo," Miguel shouted, "come into the house and see my bird!"

I followed the two boys inside. Their wild-eyed diminutive cousin Daniel—Diana's son—soon appeared behind us. The house consisted of only one room, with a cement floor and a cardboard ceiling. But they had made it into a home. Beds covered much of the floor space, and on one of them a girl of about seven and her baby sister played. Above us a wire pierced the cardboard ceiling and, looping from a naked bulb hanging loosely in the center of the room, made its way to a dangling box of outlets, crammed with wires. One of them led to a full-sized refrigerator humming loudly in the corner. Others snaked from a stack of televisions that dominated one side of the room. On the bottom of the stack was the oldest, in a large wooden case. But it had completed the transition to furniture, and the screen was turned toward the wall. Above it were two more of diminishing size. The one on top worked, roaring into action for a moment as Carlito ranged the room starting various devices, including a large boom box with detachable speakers. In the corner a collection of dozens of tiny family photos stood on a kind of sack, and on the wall hung a lone photo of the parents posing together on a beach during what must have been their honeymoon.

Around the room were the bits and pieces with which anyone would build a home—some of them, like the photos, trailing memories and hopes. The others were commodities, goods such as clothing or appliances that had, often enough, come full circle, having been assembled in some other poor city for so many cents an hour and then come to rest here on these sparse shelves, along with the consumable items that signal family life. The total effect was nearly a parody of the middle-class American home. Or perhaps a metonym, the cornucopia of consumerism represented in a few carefully chosen items.

A box of Q-tips and three jars on a shelf stood for a medicine cabinet; a sack of sugar and a box of cereal was the kitchen cupboard.

"Here is our bird!" Miguel roused me from my reverie, reminding me that however thin and fragile materially they may be, these homes are always pulsing with life. He was holding up a small cage for my inspection. Inside, a little canary hopped and warbled, no doubt accustomed to attention, for it was surrounded by the thrilled faces and poking fingers of all the children.

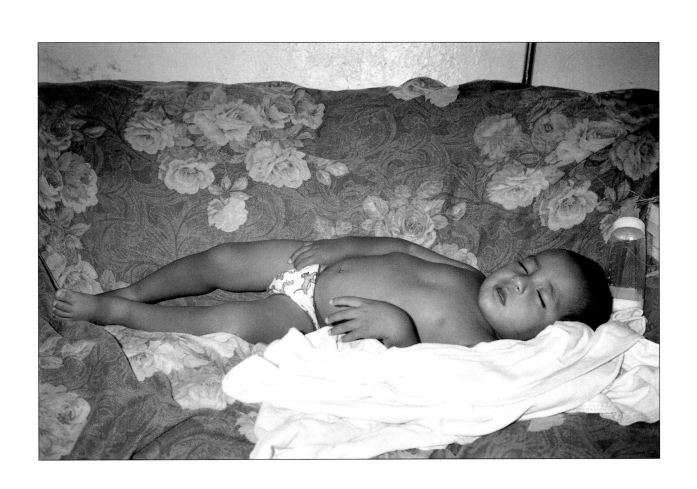

▋ LOS CHAMACOS

Por supuesto es un ángel caído, y ha
Prestado sus alas y su traje a todos los demonios.
Of course it is a fallen angel and has
Lent its wings and its costume to all the devils.
—José Emilio Pacheco

IT WAS FRIDAY NIGHT, AND ROBERTO AND I DECIDED TO GO TO "REGIS," a deep cave of a bar on one of the streets very near the border. As usual, nearly every one of the many small tables was filled with a group of young men, talking loudly and pulling one small bottle of beer after another from *cubetas*—ice-filled buckets—next to their tables. Not a single woman in sight. Not one gaily colored tile or bad painting graced the walls of that dark hall: it was all men, beer, and tequila. And music: a pair of *norteño* musicians, one with a cell phone in a holster hanging from an ostrich-skin belt, were stationed at the rear of the bar, where they belted out tunes to no one's evident appreciation.

A tall, thin boy with hazel eyes and very light brown hair entered the bar and began drifting from table to table, his swollen, dirty hands holding a carton filled with tiny packets of Chiclets.

"I know that *chamaco* [kid]," Roberto said, calling him over.

"This is El Guero"—the blond—Roberto said when the lanky teenager had joined us. I had been working with street kids for months but I had never seen one in such bad shape. He moved with the stiff shuffle of an old, sick man, his bony hands were shaking, and his eyes came and went from this world to some other.

"Are you El Guero whose *placaso* [graffiti signature] I have seen all over Nogales?" I asked.

"Yes, that is me!" he replied, brightening. "Where did you see it?"

"In the Palacio de Quemado"—I began to list the confiscated drug lords' houses, highway over-passes, park benches, and other such sites around the city that had been claimed by him and other members of the gang Barrio Libre—the Free Barrio. "And in the tunnel," I said, concluding with the most important place, the defining territory of the several dozen members of that band.

He leaned over, clearly happy to have found a sympathetic audience, and glanced toward the pack of cigarettes on the table. Roberto offered him one. El Guero lit up and leaned back; his hands shook less as he spoke.

51

"So, you have been in the tunnel?" he asked. "I have been going there for three years. Do you know Chito? Do you know El Negro?"

He went on to list more of his compatriots, most of whom I knew well.

"And did you see the newspaper story about the tunnel last year, with the photos? Well, it was I who took them through the tunnel. That's right—guided them through so that no one would harm them."

I knew the story he was talking about. Over the past four years, a smattering of television and newspaper accounts had appeared about these kids and the tunnels in which they sometimes lived and worked. They were two large storm drainage passages under the border that carried everything imaginable from Mexico to the United States. The stories began when the kids started popping up on the U.S. side of the tunnels, mugging people around a few fast-food restaurants a mile into Arizona. Graphic descriptions depicted wild, violent "tunnel rats" stoned on spray paint and harder drugs— "Lord of the Flies" fantasies that caught the fearful imagination of viewers and readers. One journalist, getting the story backward, called them "vampires" and had them sleeping in the tunnels by day and then coming out at night to rob the people of the colonias. In fact, when added law enforcement efforts on the U.S. side curbed their mugging enterprise there, they turned mainly to both guiding and robbing immigrants, who began to use the tunnels as the Border Patrol applied greater pressure to the fences. The kids slept in the tunnels because they were theirs, because these were the last places left to them.

I asked Guero where he had come from, and he told one version of a story I heard dozens of times. He had left home in Navojoa—two hundred miles south—at the age of ten and come up on the rails. He had already been a street kid at home, escaping from a family that had broken under the strain of poverty and misfortune. By the age of ten, he was making a living washing windshields and selling pills. Hearing that more money was to be made on the border, he reached the same decision that adults were making. His every move, it seemed to me, had been rational—a sensible decision given the possibilities—and yet together they had led him to this point: seventeen, addicted to God knew how many drugs, sickly, and selling Chiclets in bars.

"The tunnel is very hot now," he said. "It is crawling with cops—Betas—but I will take you down there if you like."

54

WE WERE DRIVING SLOWLY THROUGH THE SATURDAY NIGHT STREETS OF NOGALES, past thumping discos and brightly lit taco stands. Everybody was out: *vaqueros* in their best lizard-skin boots and big white hats, young *maquiladora* workers out to forget the week with beer and cocaine, packs of jiving hustlers doing deals on every corner, and, of course, prostitutes. Unlike some Mexican border towns, Nogales has no defined and controlled *zona rosa*, and the business of sex, like that of drugs, seems to go on everywhere downtown. Like the bars, the prostitutes were there to serve every client niche. One block was "transvestite central," another home to the skinny skag queens, and behind a wall were the "full-figured" *mamacitas* teetering on high heels. Stopped by the traffic, I looked out the window at two young hookers swaggering down the street arm in arm. One of them was in the shadows, but the other was illuminated by the streetlights, long brown legs and white-frosted lipstick shining in the night. She turned toward us, broke into a smile, and ran over to the car.

"Lorenzo, Mah-aye-ba," she nearly shouted with glee, leaning in through the window.

"Linda!" we exclaimed in unison. I was stunned to recognize the sultry beauty in short shorts as a fifteen-year-old girl we knew. We had met her a few weeks earlier at the homeless kids' shelter when we had picked up Lupita, a street kid we had been working with, for a weekend trip to the seashore. Linda had emerged with her, clutching her luggage—a tiny plastic shopping bag of clothes. She had been as surprised to see us as we were her. On the way down she had said little, mentioning only, as we passed a large building with a fenced yard, that she had met Lupita there, "in El Cotume [the juvenile detention center] last month." She had fallen silent again until we passed a sprawling tourist hotel on the southern outskirts of the city, when she had turned to Lupita to tell her that she had stayed there once—with a customer.

During our two days in Puerto Peñasco, Linda had floated in and out of her reveries. But the sea—which she had seen there for the first time, although she had grown up not far from the coastal city of Los Mochis, Sinaloa—seemed to give her back a fleeting childhood. She and Lupita had walked along the beach holding hands, letting the surf lick their feet. By the time I returned shoreward from a long swim, they were laughing hysterically, letting the waves roll them over and over in the wet sand. Later that evening, Lupita recalled that she had been taught that menstruating women should not swim in the sea. "Yes," Linda had replied, "the sea would be angry—fishermen might drown. Do you think that can be true, Mah-aye-bah?" she had asked. "Bien posible," Maeve had replied, much to their surprise and delight.

On the way home to Nogales, Linda had remained quiet but now and again had spoken softly, as if to herself, of her past. She was, in fact, unusual among the street girls we had met, in that she had come alone to Nogales from far away. Homelessness, we had learned, was often a relative rather than an absolute condition. Some of the boys were regular "commuters" to family homes hundreds of miles away, and most of the girls came to Nogales with their families and either stayed with or at least visited them periodically. Lupita, for example, had a father and siblings in a poor but decent home in one of the colonias. But she preferred to hang out with the other kids and had for months slept in a dirt-floor

shack with her own baby and eight or ten friends. She stopped by her father's to visit with her baby, but she did not get along well with him or her siblings. Another girl we knew split her time nearly in half. If the tunnel was profitable, she might be in it for a few days at a time and then return to the shack in Colonia Cinco de Mayo where her mother would be watching the daughter's baby along with five young children of her own.

But Linda had arrived in Nogales alone and scared, running from the memory of a miscarriage she had had at home in Los Mochis, trying to find friends in a new and dangerous city. Her way of handling her fear was the stony-faced withdrawal we had seen through most of the trip. But having revealed some of the dark secrets of her past, she had risked speaking of the future, confiding in Maeve that she hoped to wed an elusive coyote she had met in the streets of Nogales.

And now she was back working the streets.

"Do you have the photos from our trip?" she asked Maeve, and then turned to her friend, who had been hanging back in the shadows, no doubt surprised and confused by our reunion. Linda beamed like any happy teenager talking about a school holiday. "We all went to the beach together," she enthused. "It was great!"

RICARDO "MALOS OJOS" (BAD EYES) AND JAIME FOUGHT LIKE TYPICAL BROTHERS, but most often they were inseparable. They were both short and a bit squat for their ages—twelve and thirteen. Jaime was dark-skinned and handsome, a beautiful round face with dancing eyes and thick black hair. Ricardo always wore a baseball cap and walked around with his head tilted back so that he could see ahead of him. He had vision only from the bottom sliver of his eyes, since an allergic reaction to penicillin several years before had coated his eyes to near-blindness.

An operation could have restored his sight, but the expense would have been considerable. Nor, according to Ricardo, was his sight his only problem. He periodically ran away from his father. "He comes home drunk and beats my mother," he told me. When I met the father, I had trouble believing that story at first—he was such a friendly fellow. That is, until Jaime crossed him and he burst forth with a torrent of screaming abuse. An American volunteer had taken on Ricardo as his personal project, trying to mediate between him and his father and writing to corporations and old friends to ask for donations toward the operation.

In the meantime, Ricardo was living his life between home, street, and shelter like the other kids. His vision was good enough to make out whether or not any pair of jeans or shirt was a Tommy Hilfiger, and he roamed the dusty streets of his colonia with brother, cousins, and friends looking for fun and sometimes trouble. He was as up for anything as any of the kids, and most of the time he followed along uncomplainingly—even if his vision made whatever they were doing difficult for him. Rarely, he found himself stymied by his affliction, and then he would grow sullen and lose his temper. If Jaime was around, Ricardo would pick a fight, and his brother would happily oblige. Some shouting and shoves and it would all be over, with the required letting off of steam.

One day I found Ricardo loafing about the shelter, bored and disconsolate. The dead air and lack of activity there often induced that state, so it was hard to know whether anything in particular was wrong. I had brought a video camera with me, hoping to interest a few of the kids in making a film together. Frankly, I had not thought of Ricardo, and seeing him sulking there I hesitated to introduce a new activity from which he might be excluded.

But before I could say anything, Ricardo was at my side, his head tilted back and his hands shooting out for the camera. I explained its use, and in seconds he had flicked out the screen and pushed the record button. As it turned out, I had a video model particularly well suited for him, as it had a large viewing screen that he could hold directly up to his eyes while swiveling the lens to film anywhere he wanted. Far from being an obstacle, the camera became a kind of portable window for him. Like any other Mexican, he went straight for the youngest child—a baby girl, the third child of a seventeen-year-old mother. Little Clara bubbled obligingly as Ricardo pointed the lens inches from her face. He laughed and then filmed the mother. Then the other kids. Finally, possessed by a kind of euphoria, he began to run from room to room, shouting and filming everybody and everything, as if he had never seen them before.

65

66

▮ LA LÍNEA

Temo que la verdadera frontera
la trae cada uno adentro.
I'm afraid that each of us carries the real frontier inside.
—Carlos Fuentes

WE WERE WALKING IN COLONIA BUENOS AIRES WHEN I SAW A COP leaning his consider-
able weight against a gate in front of what appeared to be a large, empty stone house facing the border
fence. It was the last home on Calle Internacional; the street there gave way to a concrete stairway
rising up the steep hill to the east. The cracked and weedy steps paralleled *las láminas,* as the fence of
corrugated metal landing strips, recycled from the Vietnam War, was popularly known. A few houses
were visible on the hillside, but then the stairway, dirt paths, and border fence all disappeared over the
rise. The *municipale*—recognizable by his brown uniform—looked bored and friendly, so I walked over
to ask him what was going on.

"I am guarding this place," the cop said amiably, jerking a thumb over his shoulder, "una casa confiscada de un narcotraficante"—the confiscated house of a drug trafficker. "We took it a few weeks ago,
but we haven't got the owner! Now we have to watch it to see that he doesn't sneak back."

Or anyone else, I thought, thinking of our friends the street kids, for whom these *confiscadas* often
served as clubhouses and sleeping quarters for as long as they could manage to squat in them. These
sometimes palatial homes were scattered about the city, some of them in the wealthy neighborhood of
Colonia Kennedy but many in the poorest areas: brick, stone, or cement-block mansions amid the
shacks and trash heaps.

I asked if he saw much action around the fence, telling him that on a visit there a few years earlier
we had watched people pouring through a hole cut in it. "I watched people from one of those houses up
the hill," I told him, "who must have had a business doing that. The emigrants waited patiently in a line
that stretched down the stairway. And a lookout surveyed the scene from the top of the fence. Every
time the coast was clear, another one or two people would crawl through the hole and then slide down
the grassy hill on the American side, clutching their few belongings and disappearing into the streets of
Nogales, Arizona."

"That's right!" the policeman answered, smiling at his countrymen's enterprise. "There was a lot of action there then. Less now. The fence is better guarded than it used to be—at least right there. Now more cross in the tunnels—and farther out in the desert." He was no longer smiling. "But that is bad, because there it is very dangerous."

In fact, people died regularly trying to cross the desert. So far that summer the tally was nine, a typical season. On the fence, just yards away, a sign warned would-be immigrants of the dangers of such an attempt in temperatures that regularly topped 110 degrees. And I had seen newspaper articles, even little posters in bar rest rooms throughout the city, carrying similar warnings. More realistically, the posters would end with a list of necessities for those determined to make the journey despite the dangers. Unscrupulous coyotes would lead a party out in the desert borderlands, where the fence was a few inconsequential wires, and leave them to find their own way. Or else a few stragglers, who could not keep up with the rest, would stop for their last drops of water only to find that the party had disappeared over the sand hills while they were rubbing their burning feet.

"Do you like Nogales? Do you like Mexico? Don't you find it too dirty and noisy here?" the cop asked me suddenly. Perhaps he was thinking of why people left—or wondering why I was there.

"I do like it," I replied truthfully. "It is dirty and noisy, but it is very lively. And I have always liked the people and life of Mexico."

That was clearly the right answer. "My name is Miguel," he said offering his hand in friendship. We shook, and then leaned back, side by side, against the massive stone gate. Miguel stared back at the fence for long moment and then continued, "I spent time over there. I had a card and everything—legal. I made money all right, but I couldn't get used to the place. The streets would be empty at night. Empty. At first I thought, how peaceful! But then I began to miss the noise!" He laughed, draping a hand across his belly. Then he frowned and said, "And the people were just not warm. Not friendly. If they didn't know you, they didn't want to know you. I am talking about the Mexicans over there—the Mexican Americans! Anyway, after a couple of years I decided that I had had enough and I came back here. Now I have a decent job. The pay is OK. But mainly I prefer the life—even with the noise and filth!" He gave a self-satisfied chuckle.

"By the way," I said, "We were thinking of going up the stairway here, to see more of the colonia. Is it safe?"

I followed him a few steps to the foot of the stairway, where he stood silent for a moment, looking up the hill. "You can go as far as that white house there," he said, pointing to the third home along the vertical pathway—maybe two hundred yards above us. "Beyond that is 'no-man's-land,' as you would say. There I cannot guarantee your safety. I wouldn't go there myself with this gun," he said patting his holster. "Not without several other cops." He paused and chuckled ominously. "No, not even then!"

WE MET ROBERTO JUST AROUND THE CORNER FROM *LA CASA CONFISCADA,* on Canal Street, a strange place in the light of day. The bars were open, but where Nogales, Arizona, high-school students had been knocking back beers the night before under the smiling eyes of owners catering to that lucrative trade, now only a few seriously grubby locals were slumped on their stools nursing Pacíficos. Roberto emerged from one of the shadowy doorways, bone thin and walking quickly, his black curls bouncing as he turned his head nervously in all directions. He was armed, as always, with his guitar.

"Poor Nina," he said massaging the guitar case, "she was working for me very late last night. Anyway, it's good that she and I have jobs here, too." He threw his head back and smiled. "Now, it would be perfect if only someone would pay!" He laughed good-naturedly, his half-crazed black eyes dancing. "Anyway, you wanted to see the border, and so I'll take you to see a real border person—an artist friend of mine who lives in Arizona and has a studio in Mexico."

The mirror image of Roberto, I thought, who lives just south of the border in Mexico but works in Arizona. Real *fronterizos*. In Roberto's case, home was a tiny apartment in La Reforma, an inner-city neighborhood whose gang by the same name had inscribed many walls with its collective and individual signatures. Roberto's workplace was only a mile up the road, but in a different country. Although he had a permanent resident card for the United States, Roberto had made the economically rational choice of renting in Mexico. He was paying less than one hundred dollars a month for two rooms in a small but complicated old building of crumbling azure plaster. But he had been burgled three times in the past few months and was beginning to calculate the losses as part of the rent. "If I could share an apartment with some friends on the other side," he said—referring to the United States in the way everyone does here—"it might work out cheaper in the end! Anyway, I know which one of my neighbors is doing it. In fact I was out last night, drunk, screaming at the bastard, telling the whole fucking neighborhood that I knew what was going on."

As I wondered what Roberto could do with such knowledge, he led us through the still sleepy late-morning streets of the district to a pink plaster building on a corner. It looked like a defunct shop. Roberto's friend David ushered us into a series of bare rooms illuminated by streaming desert light. Everywhere were large canvases covered with bold and bright, or sumptuously dreamy, figures: the work of two of the three artists who shared the studio.

"We are here because it is cheaper," David told us with a wry smile, bending his delicate, finely turned head to survey the paintings he was about to ship to an exhibition in Las Vegas. "That is the case for Miguel and me," he continued. "The other artist, Fernando, lives on this side. He is from here."

"Are you and Miguel from the other side?" I asked.

"Both sides," he answered smiling. "It can be hard to say and hard to tell. But that, I suppose, is the charm of this border life, and another reason—beyond the rent—that I like to live on one side and paint on the other."

I found David's life an even more interesting artistic piece than his paintings. It was certainly more complex and ironic. If art aims to undermine the taken-for-granted, then the border seemed to do that by its very existence. But David's daily movements at once acknowledged, even helped perform, the "reality" of that border, even as they subverted its ability to define and contain him. And most strangely, each aspect seemed to reinforce the other. The more he cooperated in the creation of the border, the more powerful his subversion. The more effective the subversion, the more "real" the thing or idea subverted.

But such a philosophic view cannot always be sustained in the face of grim customs agents or immigration officers intent on reducing all ambiguity to simple yes or no questions about who you are and what you are carrying. So we were reminded a few hours later as I drove Roberto to his job in the United States.

We were sent over to the inspection bay. Roberto and I were asked to step out and away from the car as the team of agents, armed with long-handled mirrors and a huge drug-sniffing German shepherd, circled it, poking and prodding everywhere. Roberto was getting nervous—not because we were carrying anything but because he feared showing up late for work once again. I was calm until the dog was sent scrambling through the open window into the car, where it proceeded to pounce, crawl, and nuzzle every corner of the interior. I cursed softly in exasperation and Roberto felt, I think, embarrassed at my treatment in his part of the world—his homeland. So he walked over to the agent in charge, a corpulent blond whose name tag read "Apple."

"You shouldn't let the dog do that. He's really messing up my friend's car," Roberto said in perfect but lightly accented English.

"He's doing his job," Agent Apple replied, staring icily into Roberto's eyes. "Let me see your card," he demanded, clearly angry at having been questioned at all, but certainly by a "foreigner."

He held the card and smiled as if it were Roberto's testicles he had in his fist. "You have a lot of nerve complaining," he said, staring into Roberto's nervous face. "This card is a privilege, not a God-given right. We could take this card away from you whenever we want!" He flicked it with his finger and walked back to the other officers, leaving us to guess whether he was in fact intending to begin a revocation procedure or was simply torturing his prey. After several minutes, the inspection was over, and Officer Apple strolled back to where we were standing, handing Roberto back his card without looking at him.

The irony of a blond guy from Wisconsin named Apple threatening to disenfranchise Roberto in the place where he grew up and where most people on both sides of the border looked like him and spoke Spanish seemed to escape the officer. For Roberto, the irony was, for that moment, only bitter. He seemed even smaller and thinner than usual, and he nearly shook with fury and humiliation as we drove away from the border and into Arizona.

MAEVE AND I WANTED TO SEE THE BORDER not only from the other side but from another perspective, so we requested a "ride-along" with the United States Border Patrol. Agent John S. met us in a sprawling new headquarters not far from the new truck crossing point on Mariposa Road, and we followed him into one of dozens of new patrol cars sitting in the parking lot. John was a reserved but friendly young man, an Anglo from the Midwest with a smattering of classroom Spanish. He had come to the area eleven years before and seemed happy enough for a break in his routine patrol duty.

"Usually, I'd be going out through the desert, to the west of the city. It can be very quiet there, though. I thought you two would rather see action, so we'll go on into town, if that's all right." We were happy with the decision and settled in for an all-day cruise.

The scene for the Border Patrol had changed a lot in recent years, as John told us on our way toward town. "Up till maybe seven years ago, there was no fence at all, or only a few straggly strands regularly put aside. There were few agents then, and the people just went around the town, just past the fence. Then, when they put up the corrugated landing mats, that pushed the people a bit further out of town and they started going over that fence. And into the tunnel."

The situation in Nogales was merely a microcosm of the larger picture. The U.S. government's response to the increasing flow of illegal immigration over the last few years had never been to allow the same "free market forces" to work as it was encouraging under NAFTA. Rather, the answer had always been to increase enforcement and erect more, and higher, barriers. And of course to put more enforcers in the field. Between 1995 and 1998, the Border Patrol hired five thousand new agents, of whom only three thousand stayed on. Apparently, it is not an easy job. In the San Diego sector, the most active and the most difficult, one agent quit every day during that period. But it has not been clear that more agents is the answer, and in June 1999, the U.S. Immigration and Naturalization Service—the INS, *la migra*—announced that it wanted to slow down hiring. Politicians hoping to appear "vigilant," however, insisted on a 1996 provision that required the hiring of one thousand agents a year through 2002, and the U.S. Senate appropriated $83 million for that purpose. More ominously, the Senate also approved legislation that would allow the attorney general or treasury secretary to dispatch army troops to the border. This, despite a strong feeling in the Pentagon and among many actually involved in enforcing the border that deploying troops would be a mistake. Not to mention the misgivings of those who live in this part of the country. Many were still reeling over a 1997 incident in Redmond, Texas, where, their presence unknown to locals, Marines on covert maneuvers in the hills surrounding the village shot and killed an eighteen-year-old Mexican American while he tended his goats.

Looking out the window of the Border Patrol vehicle, I could not help thinking that in some ways it was too late to talk about the merits of militarization. Nogales already looked like a police state or, perhaps even more so, a territory occupied by a foreign power. The Constitution could be suspended anywhere near the border. In their pursuit of either drugs or illegal immigrants, Border Patrol agents were not required to respect "private property" and needed no warrant to search any car or home in which they suspected illegal people or substances were hidden. Dozens of Border Patrol cars cruised through town at any given moment, along with bicycle and foot patrols. It was literally impossible to go anywhere without encountering half a dozen. And they were always busy: the number of arrests was staggering. The figure for the Tucson sector of the border—which included both Nogales and Douglas, another border town to the east—was thirty-one thousand in July 1998: a thousand people a day.

John cruised along the border fence in the center of town, inspecting the new, decorative section that had been added recently, and then turned north up the main business thoroughfare, Morley Avenue: La Morley. Up until 1994, this place had been a major attraction for Mexican nationals— those living in the "border zone" were issued "Frontier Cards" that permitted quick passage for a limited time. Every day the street had been crammed with Mexican shoppers, the wealthy buying Rolexes and designer clothing, the poor searching through bins of household articles and shelves stacked with cheap electronic gadgets. The signs were in Spanish, and the shop owners were often either Jews or Koreans. The former had been in the town since its founding; the latter had followed Chinese merchants who themselves had arrived not long after the Jews. But then came the big peso devaluation in 1994, when the exchange rate went overnight from three pesos to nearly six pesos per dollar. The loss of business was immediate. Since then, the downward trend had continued, and as of the summer of 1999, the peso stood at more than nine to the dollar.

Even though the shops were far less busy than a few years before, the streets we cruised with John were far from deserted. Since nearly everyone on them was of Mexican descent, I wondered how he, or any other agent, could tell whom to stop.

"I keep my eyes open for whatever is out there. You're looking for people. You're looking for 'activity.' The people who look at you going by"—I saw many such, nervously noting our passage—"they are not the ones you stop. It's the ones who won't look at you. And of course you can tell a lot from the way they are dressed. People who are from here—from either side of the border—wear T-shirts and other things I'll recognize. The ones from further south don't. Their clothes have a different look."

We turned west and up a steep hill lined with modest but charming houses—some wood frame, others brick or adobe in azure blue or soft pink. The side of one house was decorated with the ever popular Our Lady of Guadalupe in its local, tile mosaic form. But John was looking for other things. "This area—Short and East Streets—is one of the hottest, if not *the* hottest, in the city," he said.

"In what sense?" I asked him.

"Drug activity. Illegals regularly come through here—but they are not usually dangerous. I did have a rock thrown at me once, but generally speaking, it's the drug runners who are going to be armed and violent. Most of what comes through here is marijuana. Though we do get some cocaine now and again."

We pulled over on a rise from which the border fence was plainly visible a few hundred yards to the south.

"I don't want to stay parked here too long," John said. "I never feel that it's too safe to do that in this neighborhood. I just keep moving. But look over there." He pointed with his binoculars to a section of the fence. "Here, take a look."

Through the lenses, I saw a man sitting atop the fence. Then others started to appear next to him. A woman in a skirt was lowered by brown arms. Her purse was sent down after her. Then her baby. Then a man.

I wondered why John wasn't snapping into action.

"Officers have different styles," he said. "Some will rush right in, but many will kind of hang back and watch the movement, waiting till they filter out to the road or path. You see, people like that don't have many choices. Once you've been through this you'd nearly know where they'd go next." While we watched, John's radio was crackling with information about this very episode, for another Border Patrol "unit" had, in fact, "rushed right in" and was sitting only yards from the would-be immigrant party.

"We need an ambulance," the voice on the radio said. "There's a man down with a compound fracture. I am going to stand right next to the fence; they have less chance of hitting me here . . . He's in really bad shape," the voice repeated, more urgently. "Send an ambulance, and make them hurry!"

We continued to watch the whole drama from that quiet distance, with radio commentary, as white birds floated serenely above the border fence. When the ambulance arrived, we pulled out and descended back into town, continuing up Morley to a small rail yard—for Mexican street kids, a favorite place for hopping a ride to Tucson.

"This right now is probably the most often used way out of the tunnel," John explained as we stood looking down into a narrow, rock- and trash-strewn, aqua blue concrete trough. It led out from a square hole, less than three feet on a side, in the cement embankment, which dropped away from the street maybe half a mile north of the border.

"Lots of these small passages branch off the main tunnel. First the authorities tried to block them off with gates that could be mechanically raised in the rains, but people would come with floor jacks to lift them up. Then they welded them shut. But then they had to take them off—after one good rain they'd be jammed with trash."

Meanwhile, two of John's colleagues had rolled up on bicycles. One of them, Mike, a handsome young man with a bitter smile, heard our conversation about the cat-and-mouse game of the tunnel and passages and added a fuller explanation.

"Yeah, the rains. This is the monsoon season and that always means more work for us. They know that the tunnels and passages have to be left open, otherwise they clog up with trash and the other side would be under water. You see, the illegals used to come up through the main tunnel. We would sit back and watch from a distance, and when people came out we would follow them and get them. But the papers stirred up everybody from around here with photos of illegals coming out of the tunnel. Then they were all demanding that we do something about it. So we began to park right at the exits round the clock. So of course nobody comes up that way anymore. Instead, they take all the side passages and come up through grates and manholes all over the city. We would need to be everywhere to catch them. But the citizens are happy because they don't see illegals coming out of the tunnel. 'If you don't see them, they're not there'—that's how they think. And that is the sorry truth." He shook his head and laughed.

I asked him if he had ever been in the tunnel himself, and whether he felt bad for those who came through them.

"I wouldn't set foot in that stinking hole. No way. It's their choice to stay or to come. That's how I see it. Bandits in the tunnel rob them every time. Coyotes lead them through, let them get robbed, and then send them out to get arrested. The coyotes themselves will sit right at the entrance. You have to be very stealthy to catch one."

82   John had been nodding in agreement throughout the speech about the tunnel game, but he seemed a bit more sympathetic to the poor folk at the mercy of bandits at one end and cops at the other.

Before they left, I asked Mike how he liked being closer to the ground. Police officers back east had told me that people found them more approachable on bikes than in patrol cars.

"I prefer being on the bike," Mike replied. "I get through town a lot faster, and I have more contact with the public and a better sense of what's going on. But as far as being friendlier . . . I guess I get both sides. People are more likely to come and say hello, but they can get in your face easier, too."

A radio call came in, and Mike and his buddy wheeled off down Morley Avenue. We continued our journey with John, first in the wild desert just beyond the city, where *las láminas* ended, replaced by a chain-link fence with several sections pushed flat to the ground. That was the other side of the Buenos Aires "no-man's-land."

"This is a wild area," John said. "You never know what you'll find. Last week, some agents ran into a group of Betas—the border cops from the other side—who had come over. Their story was that they were saving some illegals from bandits. But I heard a lot of rumors that the Betas were themselves the bandits."

We reentered the city, where John showed us more tunnel exits from which aspiring Americans had emerged during recent weeks. "Look here," he said. We were standing on the sidewalk on Grand Avenue. Beneath us, a sewer grate had been welded down with reinforcing iron bars. We peered in and saw a pipe a few feet in diameter.

"That pipe you see comes off the tunnel—maybe sixty feet or so," John explained. "One night last week, a group crawled through from the tunnel and jacked up the grate. They came pouring out, dozens of them. It was incredible." John, I thought, couldn't help a grudging respect for the intensity of effort involved. "Nothing can keep them from getting through—they'll use a big floor-jack, like you use to hold up a floor in a house, to bust through anything that's in their way. And the drug dealers are damned inventive too. They'll package the drugs to fit exactly through a narrow gutter hole and park a truck right over it, slide back the floor, and pass the drugs up.

John spent the rest of the afternoon arresting people. Following radio directions from command central—where all kinds of sensor information were being monitored—we cornered a party of seven in a neighborhood just over the fence from Buenos Aires. Five young men and two women crouched at the top of a stone stairway. John went up by himself, and they all came trooping down with him. The arrests we saw all went like that. Passive people complying silently with directions, filling out their own arrest forms, waiting patiently to be taken away.

We stood watching another agent—a local Hispanic by name and accent—load a whole family into a minivan.

"I had some from Chiapas this morning; these are from Yucatán," he told us. They were all dressed for shopping: the silver-haired father in neat slacks and shirt, his wife and their children in flowered skirts and pressed pants. When they had climbed into the van, the agent said, apologetically, "If it were up to me I would let them in. I feel bad about what they've been through. But they'll try again, maybe even tonight. Probably tomorrow. Eventually, they will make it."

Above us, thunder cracked loudly. The agent scowled at the sky. "The rains are the worst. Many will come, thinking they can cross more easily, that we will have more trouble catching them. It's not good, because they end up hurting themselves—slipping on the fence or something." He slid the van door closed on the impassive family. "Yeah," he said again. "If it was up to me I'd let them in, but I don't have any say-so."

Driving back toward headquarters, John explained more about the way the Border Patrol operated.

"All units like this one will be patrolling their sectors, either looking for their own action or following the leads and directives that come from headquarters. But when I arrest someone or a group, I can't really do anything but wait for the transport vehicle. It would be too dangerous to leave anyone in a locked car, with the heat and all here. There's really nothing you can do with them. Two or three transport units make runs back and forth to the courthouse. They pick up your arrests and take them in. With the new identification system, it goes very fast. They do an electronic fingerprint, and if they've been arrested before it will show up. The vast majority of cases are what we call VR: Voluntary Repatriation. That means we 'ident' them and take them back over the border, and that's it. If they've been arrested many times for illegal crossings, or if they are in the system as criminal aliens, then they can face prosecution—deportation or prison."

As John explained these bureaucratic procedures, I began to think about how incredibly routinized it all was. He and dozens of other agents cruised around Nogales every day, arresting hundreds of people, processing them, and sending them back over the line. It was no different from moving papers across a desk. The cat-and-mouse game of the tunnel was probably an unacknowledged relief from the boredom of the job—at least for some.

ALTHOUGH IT WAS NOT YET RAINING TWO MILES NORTH OF THE BORDER, we could see and hear the lightning piercing the dense black clouds settled over Nogales, Sonora. Suddenly, the shortwave radio chatter was interrupted by an urgent voice. "There's a man in the wash, carried from the tunnel. Any units up near the bridge at the Arroyo Motel? We can pick him up there."

"That's us!" John was quietly excited by the prospect. "Do you want to go?" It was a rhetorical question, and within a minute or two we had pulled up along the concrete trough of the Nogales Wash next to the Arroyo Motel—the first to arrive at the scene. Maeve and I stood next to John, staring along the wash in the direction of Mexico, but not a drop of water disturbed the stones, rags, and trash that lined its bottom.

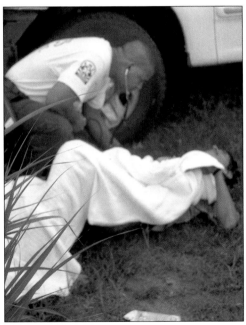

I began to think the radio dispatcher must have been mistaken, when suddenly, as if on cue, a wall of deep brown water came roaring out of nowhere like a biblical punishment, churning and roiling through the wash. In this raging, trash-laden tidal wave, everything from boards to tires bobbed and rolled. Among it all was a man. He seemed to be riding the surf, and for one bizarre moment he stopped, sitting upright in the rapids. In another instant, the waters had dislodged him and carried him on like a helpless doll toward the bridge.

Meanwhile, John had run across to the other side, joining a cop and a fireman who had since arrived there. The three of them scampered carefully down the embankment, holding hands so that John could edge down the steep slope to a position just above the water. With his free hand, he threw a bright yellow line over the water just as the man passed. The Mexican rolled in the water, reaching wildly for the line but only grazing it. His desperate face disappeared in the quickening surf. I was sure he was lost.

But I had not noticed the arrival of another team of firefighters and Border Patrol agents who had in the meantime lowered a line from the bridge that spanned the wash. As the poor man reached the bridge he weakened and sank once again into the roiling waters, but in another second the men on the bridge pulled the line taut, raising it from the water—along with strips and globs of trash and debris, and one human being. They had netted him, like an elusive bass. Everyone there cried out with relief.

As he was hauled carefully up, the man's battered jeans and underpants gave up and slid off. A fireman and a Border Patrol agent settled the nearly naked, shaking, skinny man on a guard rail and looked at him with wonder. In another moment he would have been dead, but there he was, alive and even conscious—trying, in fact, to pull his pants up from his ankles. John and the other agents, fire-fighters, and local police walked around patting each other on the shoulders.

When the paramedics laid the poor man down on the grass and covered him with a blanket, I suddenly became aware of the incredible stench of the water that had carried him, along with sewage and trash of every description, into the United States. It was a revolting scene. John walked back to us, rubbing his forearms. "Look," he said, showing us angry rashes covering both his arms. "I'm a bit sensitive to the contaminated water," he explained. "I'm afraid I am going to have get back to head-quarters and shower this off and put something on it." As uncomfortable as he was, I could not help noticing that John seemed happier than he had been all day.

WE WALKED THROUGH THE PEDESTRIAN GATE INTO MEXICO, past the customs agent, a dozen men offering taxis, a series of *taquerías*, and a newly set up row of stalls where Indian women— "Marías," the locals called them—sold everything from pots to scapulars and other magico-religious items. A local favorite was an amulet containing a picture of Jesús Malverde, a reputed Sinaloan thief believed to have been hanged in 1909 and in recent years a favorite "saint" for *narcotraficantes* and others needing protection against the forces of the state. All this activity took place up against the border fence: *las láminas*. Across the street lay the cool, gaily tiled oasis of Elvira's Restaurant, where tourists and local businessmen enjoyed some of the best regional cuisine.

Carlos, one of the waiters at Elvira's, came out to greet us, asking if we were still working with the homeless kids. We told him that we were, and he asked whether we had heard what had happened the day before.

"Right there in the road," he said, pointing in front of us. "Do you see that grate there? Below it one of the tunnels passes."

We all stood over it, staring down into the blackness. Carlos continued, "We had a lot of rain yesterday, you know, and I was out on the sidewalk wondering whether we would have to put sandbags in front of the door, when I heard yelling coming from here. Well, it was people! And when I looked down I saw them—a whole family—hanging from the bars! The water was rushing under their feet and I suppose if they had let go, they would have been swept away. 'Hold on!' I told them, and I ran back and phoned the police. Then the firemen came and eventually they got the grate out with all of them still clinging to it! Can you imagine?"

We could. Only because we had seen enough to know that any such event was not only possible but common. One of the tunnel entrances was right there in front of us—a gaping mouth clogged with mud, sewage, and broken debris of every description. Many of the kids we knew spent half their lives down there, often robbing families like the one Carlos had helped to rescue.

We went around the corner to another of our favorite restaurants, La Cebollita—the Scallion—a great place to eat and catch up on the latest episodes of the *telenovelas*, the Mexican soap operas that were always playing on the television perched on a shelf there. We would watch with the owners and soon enter into a lively discussion of the always steamy plots. But the food was the big attraction. It was to difficult to walk through that neighborhood without giving in to the temptation to sit down to a *molcajete*, a brilliant Aztec dish of seared meat, chiles, scallions, and melted cheese cooked and served in a Mexican mortar, along with a basket of corn tortillas. After a few satisfying mouthfuls, I asked the owner whether she had witnessed the rescue scene around the corner.

"Ay! Did I see it?" The wide-eyed Carlota leaned over the table, rolling her hands with emotion. "They brought them in here! To give them a meal." She smiled despite herself at the implied compliment. "So in they came—but they were so filthy! We had to send them one at a time to the *baño* to get them cleaned up. And then they ate—they ate and ate. The poor creatures! The little children they had with them, can you imagine? I scolded the parents for that. 'Take whatever chances you want, for yourselves,' I told them, 'but you can't do that to the children!'" Carlota wandered off toward the kitchen, shaking her head all the way. I had not seen her so emotional since the heroine of *Esmeralda* regained her sight.

FORTIFIED BY THE MEAL, we headed out for another border walk, continuing west on Calle Independencia. I found this end of town even stranger than the Buenos Aires "no-man's-land." It was the apparent normality that was so disconcerting. Behind the pleasant and modest homes on the north side of the street were tiny yards, each filled with utterly normal objects such as toys and garden implements. It could have been a street anywhere in Mexico, but for one surreal element. The houses shared a continuous backyard fence in the form of a ten-foot-high steel barrier: the international border.

We walked slowly down the street, greeting friendly adults and children in what began to feel like a rural village.

"Hola!" The greeting came from a heavyset man of about sixty who was ambling down the path from his front porch for a closer look at these unlikely visitors. He paused to toss a few rocks at a neighbor's dog.

"Hay muchos perros por aqui"—there are a lot of dogs around here—he laughed. "What brings you here? Are you lost?"

We told him that we were looking at the border, wondering what it must be like to live so close by it.

"It's quieter now," he said. "A few months ago many people crossed here. There was a hole in the fence and you would see them all the time, maybe twenty or thirty looking for that hole. At night. In the day. All the time. You should go further along—I'll take you just up the road to where my daughter used to work; she still keeps her car there." We fell in next to him, and together we strolled farther west, past the last houses to a low, boarded-up brick building.

"That was a radio station, up until last year," the man explained. "My daughter's car is over to the side." He pointed to a shocking pink Cadillac limousine sitting low in the yellow dirt. "She rents it out for occasions" (even with its chrome strips missing? I wondered). "If you're having a party or anything, give her a call!"

We promised we would, and the tour continued. "Look up there now and you'll get a good view and picture of the fence." He trailed Maeve and nearly pointed her camera for her. Our work done, he invited us back to his house for a cool drink. We followed him past his own porch, where we were joined by his round and equally friendly wife, and were shepherded up the steps beyond, which led to his son's more modest dwelling. On that steep slope, as elsewhere in the city, layers, tiers of houses perched on the many bare dirt hills, reached by any combination of private and public stairs, slippery slopes, and stone footholds. I remembered that the paper had recently announced a state grant to repair several dozen such cement "escalates" throughout the city. The one we climbed held till we reached the son's house.

He was already on the porch, surveying the scene over the fence and eyeing with friendly curiosity the strangers his mother was bringing up the last few steps while his father restrained the hundred-pound, five-month-old "pup." The old man hoped that the dog's youthful exuberance wouldn't keep him from terrifying the thieves and assassins who, he assured us, peopled the houses above. Looking up, you believed him. The farther your eye traveled, the more shacklike and wild the houses appeared. But here, as everywhere else in the city, that rule was broken by the sudden appearance of the apparently out-of-place sprawling brick house, always explained as the property of *narcotraficantes*—none of whom, it seemed, felt the need to move himself out of the poor neighborhood he ruled.

So we all stood on the porch—joined by a five-year-old grandchild, Lourdes, and her pet cat, Lolita —talking about the changing patterns of escape through the fence and about the constant passage of *la migra* on the dirt road that ran along it on the other side. All barely a hundred feet from where we stood.

"I was born in this house," the older man told us, "but I am a citizen of the U.S. and worked for nine years in Kmart. I picked up some English there." He used a few phrases, which we complimented, and his wife then commented that our Spanish was very good. We asked whether she spoke any English herself. "No," she said. After a long pause, she added, "But I would like to learn to speak French."

"Yes," her husband continued, still thinking about his time in the United States, "I am retired now, and I prefer to be retired here."

Our eyes turned again to the fence, watching it the way you would watch a river waiting for a trout or salmon to jump. "Look," the younger man said, pointing to a spot about two hundred yards back toward the center of town. A man was straddling the top of the fence, staring down the dirt road on the American side—a lookout for *la migra*. We looked below him just in time to see three men, one after the other, disappear into the fence. There must have been a new hole.

"Imagine," the mother said to us, patting her granddaughter's head as she spoke, "the poor people who live by the wall." She spoke as if those unfortunates were hundreds of miles away, rather than just across the street. "The noise and danger they endure with all the *migrantes* making it to America through their backyards!"

Her husband shook his head in commiseration. "No wonder some of them have put up their own fences in front of *las láminas*. They are hoping to make their yards a little less inviting than their neighbors' are."

ONE LAST BORDER ADVENTURE AWAITED US THE NEXT MORNING.

"People are not the only living things that are taken across, you know. Come with me and I'll show you both how cattle come to this country." The offer had come from Mati, another frontier woman—*una fronteriza*. A self-taught English speaker and bookkeeper, she had been born to an upper-class, rural Sonoran family of mixed European heritage and had come to live in the U.S. many years before. Her younger sister, Claudia, was a volunteer and board member for the tunnel kids' shelter, Mi Nueva Casa. Mati saw no reason to retire, and while Claudia was going over the border into Mexico with groceries for the homeless, she was busy working for the local cattlemen's association, keeping track of the passage of cattle moving in the other direction.

We arrived early that morning, climbing a dirt road up a hill, just yards from the new truck crossing at Mariposa Road. Below us, semis loaded with Sonoran grapes rumbled continuously through the gate. Above, we wandered around the corrals and chutes of another, older economy. And another, older social world as well, of Anglo and Mexican American cattle dealers discussing the week's prospects over coffee and doughnuts. They were speaking the same language—Spanish—and wore the same costume of jeans, white shirts, and of course cowboy boots. The boots were from just down the road and across the line, as a matter of fact, from the Paul Bond Boot Company, an American-owned factory manned by Mexican workers. We had gotten a tour a few weeks earlier from an elaborately polite sales assistant called Spider. The cattlemen were amused and happy to pose for Maeve's camera, and then we all filed out to the corrals, where we watched through clouds of dust as herd after herd of cattle was driven through a narrow gate by shouting vaqueros on horseback.

"When they are sprayed over there," Mati explained, pointing to the last of a maze of corrals through which the cattle passed, "they cross over. After the bath, they are Americans!"

95

■ THE AMERICANA HOTEL

Por estes callejuelas
Ancestros invisibles
Caminan con nosotros
Invisible ancestors
Walk with us
Through these back streets
—Homero Aridjes

THE NIGHT BEFORE, TAFFETA BRIDESMAIDS HAD SWIRLED TO THE BAND in the ballroom while children darted in and out of the lobby, the whole business performed under the watchful eyes of a couple of tuxedoed armed guards posted in the corners as unobtrusively as could be managed. A classic border wedding. The bride was from Tucson and the groom from Hermosillo, one hundred fifty miles south into Mexico. In the early hours, the wedding couple had headed north, along with many of the Tucson guests, but those from Hermosillo had spent the night in the hotel and now, nearly noon the next day, were nowhere to be seen.

But the hotel was busy, for it was the Fourth of July, and the steaks were already sputtering on a row of huge grills set up poolside for the occasion. I was stretched out on the patio along with several of the long-term guests; the staff shuffled amiably about, still recovering from the wedding. Tilting the umbrella against the rising sun, I lay back again and, turning a groggy head, squinted into the light toward Colleen and Sarah. They were busy smearing thick white lotion on their bodies, as they had every day that summer.

"I've always had a good body," Colleen announced, as much to herself as to Sarah. She checked carefully for flaws, as she would a possible purchase. She was probably telling the truth. A very pretty, tough thirty-year-old with golden hair, she must have been a cheerleading dream in high school. Sarah, a paler blond of twenty-eight from Northern Ireland, nodded assent and inspected her own body, into which she had put more silicone and hard work in the gym than had Colleen. Each was on her third marriage.

"I can't seem to get rid of this," Sarah said, poking at a spandex-wrapped roll of flesh just below breasts threatening to escape their scanty holder.

Colleen lit another cigarette and watched her seven-year-old daughter, Tiffany, splash around in the hotel pool. Her husband, Matt, and his assistant, Willy, had just emerged from their holiday sleep,

a rare day off work at the produce warehouse. Matt's was one of several dozen companies that maintained operations along the highway just north of Nogales. Trucks rumbled in and out all year, carrying the seasonal fruits and vegetables that stocked American markets, from the great chains to mom-and-pop groceries. Much of this produce came from Sonora, where agribusiness had bought up hundreds of thousands of acres and worked them with camps of laborers who had migrated from the empty villages of the south. But Colleen knew little about all that and cared even less. For Matt and the other brokers, bigger growers meant more reliable production and filled contracts. But his own company was a small one, and he was always looking over his shoulder at the competition—a few of whom were staying, as they did every summer for the grape season, in the same hotel—and at Colleen, who passed her time buying things he hoped he would be able to pay for.

"Mommy, look at Daddy!" little Tiffany squealed in delight. Matt and Willy were pacing opposite sides of the pool in their bathing trunks like low-budget wrestlers. Matt looked like what he was—a high-school football player already gone to flab in his early thirties. Willy, twenty years older, was just plain fat, comfortably huge and determined to use his physique in the sporting activity for which it was best suited: cannonballing. With the whoop of a beery teenager, he took two or three heavy bounds and then flung himself out over the pool, coming down with a great sloppy splash that delighted the children and sent a thin shower of spray as far as Colleen and the barbecue. Only a second of self-consciousness flickered across Matt's face and then he, too, launched into a frenetic run and, hurling himself through the air, clutched at his ankles. He broke the water like a falling boulder, sending streams arcing over all the pool edges. Their two heads—one with a shock of black hair and the other bald—seemed to bob in the water like talking melons, arguing about whose cannonball had been the best. Then Sarah's husband, Frank, their friend and competitor in all things, appeared without warning. He pounded across the courtyard and, grinning like a madman, hit the pool only a few feet from the others, sending a wall of water over the two melon-heads.

Happily relaxed after their cannonball competition, the three men joined me for a beer as their own steaks sizzled on the grill. We talked of the grape trade, and I recalled César Chávez. Frank, himself an illegal immigrant from Hungary (he had sneaked in through the other border, from Canada) who liked to observe that there was "another side" to the story of the Holocaust, was not inclined to brook any interference with the "free market." He had been arrested in Hungary for dealing drugs, and his approach to the grape trade was perhaps similar.

"I never would have put up with that," he said, referring to the famous events of decades earlier, when the word *Huelga!* had resounded through the farming regions of California. Chávez had led first his fellow Chicanos, along with immigrants, in a strike, and then millions of sympathizers across the nation into a famous grape boycott. It had been a crucial step in a Chicano political self-consciousness that was still growing, if slowly and painfully.

"No way," Frank continued with disdain. "I'd have had him killed. You can't have a person like that get in your way when you're trying to do business. You pay some guys a few thousand bucks to knock him off, and you get on with your affairs."

These days, the produce of California and Florida was still being picked by underpaid and poorly housed immigrants, but their compatriots were doing the same in the expanding trade south of the border. In some cases, American producers were buying up the Mexican operations, thus ensuring their own supply. The even more poorly paid and housed workers there had fewer options and were unlikely to rebel. Their only real choice was to move farther north, to cross *la línea*, the line, which was visible from where we sat by the pool, the fence dividing the brown hill at the eastern edge of *ambos Nogales*.

"If you want my opinion," Willy said, as if I had a choice, "I think they should add electrified wires to the top of the fence." He paused for effect. "Yeah," he continued, "and then they could fry every bastard climbing over it."

The produce brokers were an unexpected feature of the hotel in summer. They made themselves thoroughly at home for two or more months, filling the courtyard with barbecue grills, plastic pool toys, and their mainly indolent families. Most of them had been returning to the hotel for several years, time enough for a history of medical emergencies, famous bouts of drinking or drugging, and a series of liaisons and affairs with each other and the hotel staff.

But the hotel also played a major role in local life that its situation on the bleak highway did not hint at. The modest pool was a vital oasis in the blazing summer. Many local families would drop in for an hour or the day. Others might rent the pool for a children's party, and a few bought season passes, so that they became a familiar part of the summer scene. The most faithful of these was Teresa, a happily inert mother of three wild children. They bellowed and splashed while she lay, shimmering brown on a chaise lounge, like a beached seal, smoking cigarettes and commiserating with Sarah on their respective frustrations with their children. Teresa was a middle-class woman from Mexico City who had married a local Anglo and was raising her hellions to speak only English.

The hotel bar was another social center, attracting a number of local regulars and guests, including the Irish American parish priest, who lived in a room in the hotel and spent virtually every evening at the bar. The more prominent local families, Anglo and Mexican American both, found other places to cool off and to drink, but many of them liked to show up for food and socializing at the ample Sunday brunch buffet, and especially for holiday meals. Father's Day was a favorite, with giant pans of paella and strolling musicians happy to pause at any table to croon Dad's favorite tune. And the Fourth of July.

MAEVE JOINED ME AT THE POOL, amazed to have discovered that behind the unpretentious façade of the beauty parlor just across the hotel parking lot, the beautiful granddaughter of the Mexican film legend Pedro Infante styled hair and sold diaphanous gowns and chiffon pantsuits. We excused ourselves and went into the restaurant to wait for Claudia, who was as happy as any of the locals to make a holiday appearance in the hotel dining room. We watched her glide among the tables on her way to us, nodding greetings or pausing to chat according to a calculus of rank and relation.

"You know everybody," Maeve remarked as Claudia slid gracefully into her seat beside us.

"Well, yes," she answered, "with all my years working in the bank, and of course my family goes back a long way here."

Her family had come up from Sonora just after the founding of Nogales, and a great-uncle had been one of the first mayors on the U.S. side. They had been well-off ranchers in Mexico, and Claudia could still be brought to tears remembering the shooting death of her relative during the Mexican Revolution. She still had connections on the other side, where a cousin of hers presided over a decaying but still wonderful hacienda near the ruins of the Jesuit Mission of Cocóspera. She had brought us to it on a weekend outing, for a nostalgic visit and a spare but delicious meal served by a somewhat surly maid who had been rolling and pounding out wheat-flour tortillas in the dark kitchen when we arrived. The tour had been difficult for Claudia. Every turn and chamber had evoked childhood memories. "At least the light is still burning here," she had said, blinking back bitter tears at lost inheritance and general decay as we stood in the eighteenth-century chapel with its original altar and cross. "They say the light has never gone out since it was built, over two hundred years! I remember as a child that there was always somebody praying in the chapel. Every family had one." She had meant, of course, families like hers.

"Anyway," she continued, poking at her salad but still fluttering her long brown lashes at friends and neighbors, "I hope you like the Fourth of July here. You'll have a good view of the fireworks from the top of the hill, in the Veterans of Foreign Wars parking lot."

We enjoyed steaks prepared Sonoran style, listening to and joking with the Mexican musicians who strolled among the tables with their guitars, playing requests. For us, it was "Tú, solo tú." Outside in the enclosed courtyard, Colleen and the others continued to lounge around the pool, their bodies gleaming with oil under the high-noon sun. One might imagine that the hotel was making a determined effort to perform some tourist version of Mexico, and on the Fourth of July.

"Maeve, do you remember Chacha? You took photos of her granddaughters. Well, I went to see her this morning, not in the house near the golf course, but in the other one—over the line."

Maeve had told me about their visit to the house. It was in an old quarter of Nogales, not far from Memo's neighborhood, where peeling outer adobe walls hid and separated homes like Chacha's from the jiving, drug-dealing streets all around them. As in the Arizona home, which was done up in "suburban grand" rather than "genteel decay," one was greeted at the door by a maid who would presently serve unimportant visitors glasses of tepid but purified water. One home was surrounded by a manicured lawn, the other by trash and street thugs, but inside they sheltered the same family, the same careful, heavy marble and oak furniture. Only a few family photos distinguished their sitting room from a small hotel lobby.

"I tried to encourage her to contribute to Mi Nueva Casa," Claudia continued, referring to the homeless kids' shelter on whose board she served.

"Any luck?" Maeve asked her.

"She was very polite about it, of course, but she didn't commit herself. I am sure she thinks I'm out of my mind. Myrna is my only friend who doesn't think so, and that's because she is as crazy as I am!"

Claudia laughed at herself and recited, as she often did, "I started out a respectable, retired banker, and with this work I've been turned into a bag lady, a smuggler, and a liar!"

"By the way," she smiled, "what did you think of our adventures yesterday?"

We had gone out with Claudia and her equally respectable friend and accomplice Myrna, recently retired from a managerial position at Wal-Mart. Every week the two of them set out on an intensive version of what many local folks did—shopping the two sides of the border. But they did it for the kids' shelter, getting the most they could for the donated dollars.

On the U.S. side, we had pulled into the parking lot at Basha's Supermarket—the anchor of a strip mall similar in appearance to every other such shopping complex in the United States. Basha's was in fact an Arizona chain, and we had been in other branches farther north in the state. But this was the border, and Basha's was different: wide dingy aisles washed by a pulsating neon glare. The ladies wheeled their carts with determination, guided by a list of goods they knew to be anywhere from pennies to dollars cheaper on this side of the border. We rolled past tables overflowing with sticky doughnuts, burlap sacks of freshly picked chile peppers, stacks and stacks of flour and corn tortillas. We bypassed the popular meat counter, where lines of women stood gesticulating toward stacks of various animal feet or slices of pork rolled in almost iridescent red powdered spices. The two women never hesitated. Claudia's banker's mind ticked up any change in prices while two sets of beautifully manicured hands tossed sacks and boxes into the carts. Everywhere in the store the only language one heard was Spanish; the aisles were signed in that language as well, though English translations were sometimes appended.

That market had seemed a Mexican outpost in the United States. But many of the shops along the border—as in all the larger U.S. border towns—catered to a Mexican clientele seeking non-Mexican goods. Much of it was as likely to be made in the Far East as in the United States, and it sold in shops ranging from "Everything for a Dollar" to fine department stores. Most of the former were now owned and run by Koreans, who in recent years had been joining the Jewish families such as the Brackers, prominent retailers and politicians for close to one hundred years. The collapse of the peso in the mid-1990s had taken a tremendous toll on what had been a very lucrative trade.

But other factors contributed to the decline of this old retail quarter on the border. The Mexican day-trip shoppers seemed to follow American trends in favoring the big chains over family-run shops. Many of them mounted the free bus that waited just north of the pedestrian crossing gate, heading out onto the new highway and then into the vast parking lot of Wal-Mart.

A famous joke is told on the border. "What are the first words of English learned by Mexicans in the U.S.? 'Attention Wal-Mart shoppers!'" The joke is both true and ironic. Wal-Mart is a certainly a site in which American culture—or at least one class variant of American culture—is produced. It is a place where Mexicans learn how to be Americans. They learn it by making choices from within the large but circumscribed field of American products, the same ones that appear on the TV shows they are watching at home. But the irony of the joke is that those words may be the only ones in English shoppers will hear in the Nogales, Arizona, Wal-Mart. And if they are heard, they will almost certainly be followed immediately by a Spanish translation.

"No tengo mucha oportunidad hablar inglés aquí"—I don't have much opportunity to speak English here—the cashier had told me in the course of a brief chat while she rang up my purchases one day at Wal-Mart. She had been living in Arizona for twelve years, but with every possible entertainment, service, and friend available in Spanish, the incentives to learn English were not strong.

I had told that story to Myrna, who herself much preferred to speak Spanish—though her English was fine.

"That's right," she replied, laughing. "Even Wal-Mart has to fit into the world here! I remember when I worked there in the electronics section, every day a group of Mexican children—maybe half a dozen boys and girls of about ten years old or so—would show up. You could tell by the way they dressed that they were from the other side. Yes, you can always tell that. Anyway, these kids would arrive to watch the big bank of televisions we had there in the electronics department. The first time I saw them, I asked them how they were going to get home. 'Oh,' one of the boys said, 'vamos a esperar nuestro taxi'—we're going to wait for our taxi. And then they trooped out into the parking lot and just stood there until someone called in to the Border Patrol, reporting a group of illegals. Then the van came and picked them up and took them to the border. Back home. And then they would come again to Wal-Mart the next day."

We had all laughed, wheeling our shopping carts out of Basha's into the apparent America of strip-mall parking lot.

"Look!" said Maeve. There in the parking lot, a group of Border Patrol agents were busy prying open the trunk and doors of a battered brown Chevy Nova. We joined the small crowd watching. Finally, the trunk was popped and the floorboard ripped out. One of the patrolmen reached into the depths and pulled out a large bale of marijuana, handing it to the others. Then he reached in again and came up with another. And another. And another. His colleague was carrying out the same operation under the back seat. Bale after bale came out—a good dozen of them had been hidden in the car. "Maybe fifteen hundred kilos of marijuana," one of the agents was happy enough to tell me. But they were not terribly excited. "We get this much about two or three times a week," he told me. "We spot the car, maybe, coming down from one of the neighborhoods up by the fence—on this side." We knew the area he meant, having visited it with the Border Patrol. Some months later the Nogales sheriff was to make a spectacular drug bust in one of the homes there, finding an entrance to the tunnel under the floorboards. The next day the sheriff returned to the scene of the crime to arrest the people next door, who were also found with a house full of drugs. He knew something was going on, as he put it to the media, because the people had not come out to watch during the previous day's action.

The agent continued, "So then they drive them down here and leave the car in a parking lot until someone else comes along and picks it up. Happens all the time. This one was here overnight, so we knew what the story was." Why, I wondered, would the drug runners leave the car when they would surely know the patrol was likely to pick it up? Because it did not matter. They could afford to lose a certain percentage in this manner. It was part of the system. Part of the game. The bales were all there on the tarmac—like clowns out of a Volkswagen—and all that remained in the ripped-up trunk was a ragged little hand puppet; the patrolman was about to throw it back. "That's where the heroin is!" Maeve had joked. "You're probably right!" he answered, chuckling. He tossed it into his green vehicle.

With bags of groceries filling the trunk, Claudia had pointed the Lincoln toward the border. Like their American counterparts, the Mexican customs agents stop one in every few cars coming across and undertake anything from a cursory to a sweeping search. I have often seen the entire contents of a van—a ragged family and dozens of sacks and cases—piled on the pavement while agents picked slowly but not particularly thoroughly through them. Claudia was stopped as well. But she knew the routine, popping the trunk and handing the agent the checkout receipt, the total of which was just pennies below the legal import limit. Then we were off up Avenida Obregón to El Viachi, a supermarket remarkably similar to Basha's except perhaps for the huge pig's head sculpted of ground chorizo with olives for eyes that stared back at us from the meat counter. And the very different scene in the parking lot. Viachi's was in a massive garage, with full-time security guards who escorted shoppers to their cars as red-aproned boys wheeled cartloads of groceries for tips. Here, other items were cheaper, and Claudia and Myrna soon had massive quantities of them safely in their baskets.

Later that same day we had been back in the United States, just up the road from the hotel and the shopping center having lunch in Zula's Diner. My seat faced the window on the parking lot, where, just as I lifted my burrito, I saw a wiry little man running in a crouched position to a small van. He opened the door and jumped in. Other diners witnessed this scene as well, but apparently the van did not belong to anyone in the restaurant, so we all kept to our seats and continued watching. One after another, men emerged from the bushes around the parking lot and, keeping low to the ground, scurried to the van and disappeared within. A thousand clowns again, but this time reversing the feat of the marijuana bales. The driver backed out of his space and, turning toward our startled faces, smiled, waved, and drove away into the United States with his shipment of illegal immigrants in what looked for all the world like an empty vehicle.

The Fourth of July lunch in the hotel promised no such entertainment. We finished our steaks, still laughing in wonder at border life. "That's how we are!" Claudia said, rising to greet an old friend. "Now, please remember that we're going this evening to visit my friends on the ranch."

But we had other stops before that, beginning with a Baptist picnic.

"DID YOU HAVE A BURGER YET?" Pastor Fred beamed like a cartoon moon and waved a heavy arm toward the large table just behind him.

"We got everything you could want—hot dogs, hamburgers, baked beans, potato salad . . ."

Pure Americana. And several dozen happy customers, I thought, looking at rows of families and neighbors hunched over picnic tables, cheerfully knocking back paper-plate loads of brown and white food.

"This is my congregation," he said, still grinning broadly. "I thought I was retiring to this place, but I've never been so busy!" Clearly, busyness was next to godliness.

We knew some of his flock already. A few were from "the other side" and were apparently using their border crossing cards for more than shopping. As for the others, like the rest of the inhabitants of Nogales, Arizona, they were mostly Mexican American, and they were speaking Spanish over their burgers and salads.

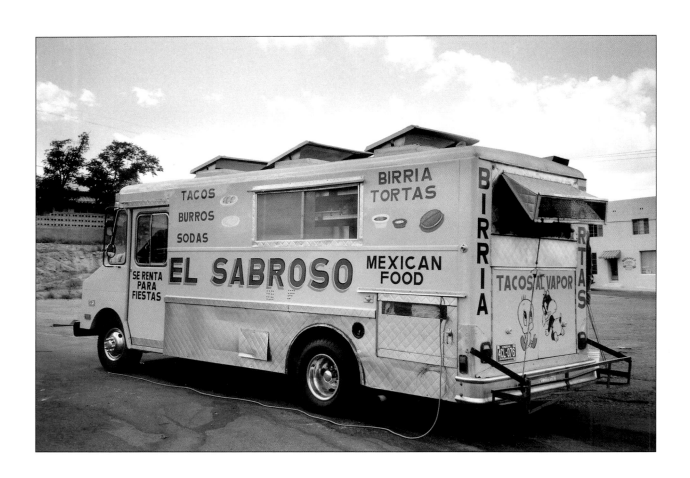

The Mexican Catholic Church, stripped of much of its property and authority after the Revolution, has not been as powerful there as it has been, for example, in Ireland or Poland. Popular religion, however, is another matter. Homemade devotional structures such as roadside shrines—particularly to that most iconically Mexican of religious figures, the Virgin of Guadalupe—are equally common on both sides of the border. Thus, if the institutional church is relatively weak, the people—particularly the poor—are thought to be profoundly Catholic, unthinkingly religious in a mysterious, superstitious sort of way. That, of course, is a profoundly Protestant point of view. But the Mexican Baptists, if their new religion has drawn them into some other place, still seem Mexican—friendly and familial around the picnic tables in a Mexican way, piling jalapeño peppers onto their burgers.

As for the American Baptists, such as the pastor and a few others we met, I am not sure whether you would want to call them profoundly religious or not. They certainly can seem unrelentingly so. Unlike Catholics, some Baptists are able to insert their religion into just about any situation or sentence imaginable. And they want to change, to improve things, situations, and people, including themselves. That makes a place like Mexico an important field of activity—a place for practicing your religion on others, thereby performing both missionary deeds and a particular version of one's self. In common with other developing world regions I have seen, parts of Mexico are allowed to become free-for-alls for those groups—often religious—that want to roam around in the space left by a state that doesn't work or doesn't want to.

The Franciscans had a mission that helped the poor in Guaymas, hundreds of miles to the south, but the Catholic Church was doing relatively little in either Nogales. The church was no doubt a more stable and even influential institution—at least a basic feature of everyday life to most families, including Claudia's—in Nogales, Arizona, than on the other side. The priest there was not, however, making a big impact on anything but the bar in the Americana Hotel.

BACK AT THE HOTEL, WE WERE GREETED BY THE MANAGER, Dr. Victor Briones (he had told us when we first met, presenting his business card with all his degrees and titles, that he was really a professor of literature), his shoe-shine-dyed orange brown hair catching the light nicely.

"You have a visitor in the lobby," he informed us with due ceremony. We made our way out to find Yvette Gonzalez Serino—whom Maeve had invited to pose—in full mariachi costume, another vision of Mexican color, standing a bit uncertainly in the antiseptic white lobby. But she broke into an irresistible smile at our appearance, and she and I wandered out into the softening late afternoon light while Maeve fetched her photographic equipment. I had last seen Yvette a few days before, dressed very differently indeed, but with the same glow, seated behind a large reception desk in the city offices lobby. Maeve had heard her perform a year before at Tucson's famous annual mariachi convention, where Yvette had stolen the show with voice, verve, and a fresh but striking beauty. As it turned out, our friend George Thomson had taught her social studies at Nogales High, from which she had recently graduated. It was he who had told Maeve where to find her at the civic offices, handling the inquiries of people she had grown up with.

"What a beautiful costume!" I said, "Do you enjoy wearing it?"

"Oh, yes," Yvette answered, laughing. "It is one of the reasons I sing mariachi."

I asked her to explain, and her answer began with family history.

"My grandparents came here from the other side, and my mother and her sister grew up here. I grew up with this music here, from so young I can't remember. My mother would sing and I would sing with her. By the time I was twelve, it seemed natural that I would sing on the stage. Not that I wasn't nervous, but I never thought about doing anything else. But my aunt, my mother's sister, she didn't approve. She wanted me to sing all right, but something 'more American.' 'Why can't you sing country and western?' she would ask me. It's true that I liked that music, too, and I would sing it around the house. But what kind of costume do you get to wear with that? No, I want to wear this!" Her eyes sparkled with laughter as her beautifully polished nails clicked over the rows of silver buttons that ran the length of black bolero jacket and long black skirt over shimmering black leather boots. She put on the great mariachi hat, the kind that hangs above tacked-up rainbow serapes on the walls of hundreds of Mexican American restaurants, and posed in the shade beside a painted cinder block wall.

After the photo session, I asked Yvette if she was often on "the other side."

"Not all that often," she admitted. "I go there for costume accessories, you see, and I did perform once on a big stage there, as an opening act for Juan Gabriel—a Mexican superstar. The crowd was great, really friendly, very enthusiastic." She paused, remembering the evening. "Actually," she reflected, "they kind of scared me. I mean, they were so loud and they kept pushing at the stage and everything, and I got really frightened. I was glad when it was over."

WE SET OUT IN THE JEEP, bouncing over rocks and ditches across the ranch. Bill kept a light hand on the wheel, describing the terrain that had been in his family for close to a century. Away from the relatively crowded houses and streets of Nogales, this was another, vaster world: the desert West, where only foot and wheel trails marked the endlessly rolling hills and momentary rivers.

We pulled over and walked along a cracked dirt path. Before us was what remained of Guévavi Mission, the ragged red adobe walls outlined against the blue sky. This was the least known and rarely visited ruin of one of Jesuit Father Eusebio Kino's late-seventeenth-century missions. The missions had once stretched from Magdalena, about seventy-five miles south of where we stood, to San Francisco Xavier del Bac, about sixty miles farther north. They had ranged along the untrustworthy banks of fleeting rivers marked by green corridors of cottonwoods in the desert, bringing Christianity, wheat, and cattle to the seminomadic natives of the region. This was the northern version of a story of conquest, cohabitation, and collaboration, the unintended consequences of which were Mexico. And that ambiguous, enigmatic nation was still here, though made yet more complex in this part of its former domain by incorporation into the United States, whose presence was felt powerfully, tangentially, or hardly at all, depending on where and with whom you were standing. Only one thing was certain: history had resolved nothing.

The sky, deep blue a moment before, was now a dense charcoal, spitting angry lightning. The rain fell with dust-splattering force, coming in undulating waves across the brown desert hills. We had returned from the mission ruins to the ranch house just in time. But in a half-hour it was over, and the fading evening light lit up the tiny wildflowers that brightened the yellow-brown sands. The sharp and distinctive smell of creosote thickened the air.

GREAT BALLS OF RED, WHITE, AND BLUE BLOSSOMED AND DIED in the northern sky. We were watching the fireworks, not from the VFW hall but from George and Liz Thomson's driveway on one of the stony dirt hills of Rio Rico, about ten miles north of Nogales. Around us were the homes of Mexicans, Mexican Americans, and Anglos—nearly all of them working in professional or managerial positions on both sides of the border. Here they had found some space and perhaps a certain distance from the line. We had joined George and Liz and some of their high-school teacher friends for a Fourth of July of beers and guitar music on this edge of the United States.

I asked George, who taught social studies, how it was possible that a large number of the Nogales teens—even those who had grown up completely on the Arizona side—spoke little English.

"Well, they speak Spanish at home, and when they come to school, they keep speaking Spanish with their friends. The bilingual program teaches them through Spanish at first and is supposed to introduce them by degrees to English. But it doesn't really work."

Indeed, I had read a newspaper account of the program, and that seemed to be the general opinion at a local Board of Education review. A local Mexican American judge had remarked that he typically found himself trying eighteen-year-olds who, although they had grown up and passed through the Nogales, Arizona, school system, required a court translator.

George continued, "After a couple of years they are supposed to be getting their instruction in English. They do, but most of them don't understand it completely, and they certainly don't speak it.

116

117

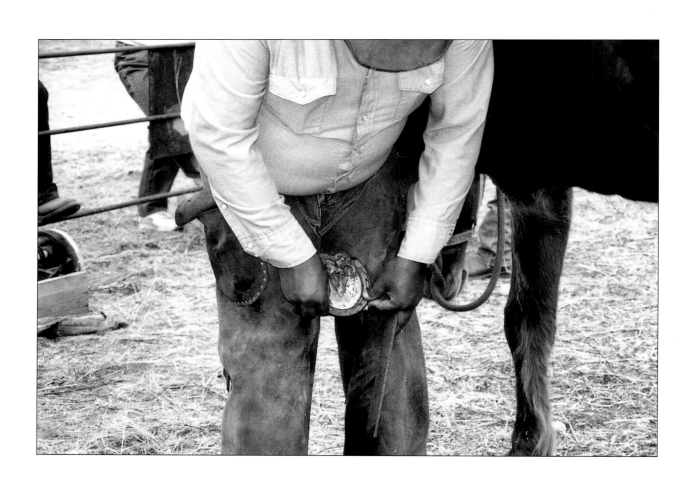

The teachers speak English and the students somehow manage, copying and so on. Doing enough to pass."

Unsatisfied with these failures, George did two things. He went to Mexico and learned Spanish himself so that he could communicate directly with his students, and he instituted a demanding senior project, requiring both written work and a ten-minute oral presentation in English.

"That's the part they dread," he explained. "For many of them, it is the single hardest thing they have to do in high school."

IN THE HOTEL THE FOLLOWING MORNING, I found a quiet place in the glassed-in lobby to write up my notes from the day before. Roberto drifted in with his guitar and a hangover, dropped onto the lobby sofa next to me, and began to sleepily pick a few desultory notes. Together we surveyed the scene outside through the wall of glass. Just beyond the parking lot was Grand Avenue, a typical U.S. commercial "strip" with gas stations and fast-food chains, in this case Church's Fried Chicken. Less typical, however, were a few other significant features—such as the exit to one of the notorious tunnels that led from Nogales, Sonora, to Nogales, Arizona. As we had seen on more than one occasion, it brought not only rainwater but also drugs and people, some of whom, like the man we had watched being rescued, continue their watery journey in the Nogales Wash. The tunnel and wash were just beneath the surface, invisible from where we sat in the lobby. But on the hills just beyond Church's, a typically uncanny scene was unfolding before our eyes. A small number of Border Patrol agents were rounding up four or five dozen people who must have just come over the fence that bisected the hill behind them. Roberto shook his head in jaded dismay.

The hypnotic low hum of the air conditioner was broken by the unlikely tones of Belfast. "Good morning," Sarah said as she parked her baby carriage and found a seat on the armchair across from us, facing the back of the lobby and the sliding glass doors that led to the protected interior courtyard and pool. "This one finally slept last night, so wouldn't you know it, of course I couldn't," Sarah good-naturedly complained, eyeing little Frank. "Anyway," she continued, "I wandered out here in time to see the all the goings-on . . ."

I looked puzzled.

"You know, who's doing what with who, and when. This place is a hotbed of activity! The girl at the desk in the mornings—the one who looks like Sonia Braga—she's been having it off with your one from Modesto. They've all been in each other's beds at one time and another. Frank was, too—he had a fling with that same Sonia one a couple of summers ago. But that was before me—though the others didn't waste any time telling me about it, just to keep me on my toes here.

"Anyway, I don't care about that. It's not the past, it's the present that's pissing me off. Like, Frank won't ever take me into Mexico. He says 'I'm not taking my family across that border—if I take them on vacation it's going to be someplace nice.' But he's over there all the time himself, not just on business, but eating and drinking with the others. They seem to have a good time there and Jesus Christ, how bad could it be? I'm from the last Catholic family on the Shankill Road in Belfast, for Christ's sake!

"How far is it, anyway—the border?" she asked, craning her neck around to look out the front lobby windows.

I laughed in astonishment, taking her over to the window and pointing over the tops of the buildings across the street. A couple of hundred yards to the southeast, the corrugated metal fence flashed in the sunlight, and the Border Patrol agents were getting the last of their catch into the transport vans.

"Just there," I said. "That is Mexico."

"Jesus Christ," she breathed. "That's another country?"

■ EPILOGUE

Fragmentos mínimos, incoherentes:
Al revés de la Historia, creadora de ruinas,
Tú hiciste con tus ruinas creaciones
Minimal, incoherent fragments:
The opposite of history, that creator of ruins,
With your ruins, you made creations
—Octavio Paz

I SUPPOSE A COUNTRY MUST BEGIN AND END SOMEWHERE.

So one might think, looking out over the city from one of the hills that enclose the valley of *ambos Nogales*. The border, however, is unconvincing; it appears simply arbitrary. Where neither sea nor river nor even mountain serves to make a boundary, perhaps anything would look as random as does that stretch of fence—sheets of corrugated metal that have already seen action in Vietnam and now divide what seems from that height to be one city. Beyond the last houses to the east and west, the fencing continues, meandering over a series of brown hills on either side. The corrugated sheets are then replaced by mere chain-link fences that, in the distance, give way to a single line of barbed wire strung from pole to pole, disappearing into the horizon.

As contingent as it thus appears, the border has even so become brutally real—an artifact of a global order that at once creates, favors, and frustrates the bottomless well of human desire that more than anything animates this place. Within the space of a few miles in either direction of "the line," all the forces that currently shape life on this earth are visible.

Naturally, both photographer and writer wonder how such a place can be discovered, represented, pictured, or imagined. People often begin with shocking figures, if for no other reason than to stun the reader with images of impossible magnitude. The border is nearly two thousand miles long; in the year 2000 about 1.5 million migrants were arrested and more than 500 perished attempting to cross into the United States. Uncounted others and untold billions in drugs did find their way across, but so did millions in legally imported electronic components, tomatoes, grapes, and on and on. Visual images are typically offered of the victims of these same colossal machinations of peoples, nation-states, and the global market—legal and illegal—in the streets of places like *ambos Nogales*. In such photos, would-be immigrants crouch against midnight fences, half-decayed bodies lie unearthed in the dumps of Juárez, and children pick through the trash heaps of Tijuana. These are the representations of the towns along the border.

All true pictures. Yet these very same cities, towns, and villages along that incredible stretch of river or desert have other lives, other stories as well. As much as border towns are subject to forces beyond their ken, each is a community in its own right, with its own history, or perhaps histories. The arid and often majestic landscape surrounding *ambos Nogales* on both sides of the border had been home to Native Americans and Mexicans for a very long time before any man-made line divided their lives. The towns, founded as trading posts late in the nineteenth century, were in fact local responses to the possibilities offered by the then new border. Local history is still a narrative of families who straddle that line and whose lives and stories have been intimately bound to one another for generations.

Even today, despite the stark and oft-noted contrast between chaotic, colorful Mexico and the relatively ordered, controlled, and structured United States, the Arizona side is in some ways more Mexican—more old-fashioned Mexican—than the Sonora side. Even though it receives a small flow of immigrants who stay, Nogales, Arizona, has not grown much, and it has a persistent social core of older families with intimate knowledge of one another, of ancient friendships and feuds. Nogales, Sonora, has such families as well, but they are vastly outnumbered by the continuous influx of migrants from the south. Though the United States has a reputation for mobility—in nearby Tucson, one quarter of the population moves every year— Nogales, Sonora, surely has a far higher rate. A 1999 official publication tells us that 350,000 people live in Sonoran Nogales, but everything there is approximate, fluctuating, vibrating. As Blanca, the resident of Colonia La Solidaridad, observed of the town, "No es un rancho, es un corral."

For the long-time resident Mexicans on both sides of the border, as much as for outsiders, that swirl of Nogales, Sonora, can be overwhelming—recall the fear of Yvette, the mariachi singer, facing the surging crowd. The color and confusion can fascinate, but more often it seems to frighten or even revolt. Señora Valdez, the woman returning after decades in the south, is not alone in feeling that Nogales, like other border towns, has become a *caricatura*, a kind of cruel joke about Mexico, and no longer Mexico itself. People remember better times lived in calmer, cleaner, less dangerous, more intimate spaces. As for Mexicans from farther afield, for them it can be a question of purity and danger. "Why not go to the *real* Mexico?" they often ask—"Why not Oaxaca?" As a Mexican diplomat recently remarked to me, "The border? I race past it! It's horrible! We Mexicans are embarrassed by it." Such people see the entire borderland as only a bastardized drug and tourist zone. If it was ever Mexico, it is some unnameable thing now. By way of proof, they are likely to point to the use of a few English words and phrases. "They don't really speak Spanish on the border," they will say.

But they do speak Spanish, of course. It is a Spanish as dynamic, as flexible, as expansive and inclusive as their lives. A purist vision of Mexico and Mexican culture can be sustained, after all, only by holding to an incredibly narrow "symbolic geography" of the country—a view hardly limited to Mexico or Mexicans, and one that would exclude the capital along with the border. And it must be said that the dynamism of border culture is very Mexican indeed. This is a people justly famous for invention and startling combination, for adopting everything from French intellectual and artistic fashions to the figures of American and global popular culture, from Mickey Mouse to Power Rangers, and casting all of them in their own Mexican show. Nor is that creative play of popular street culture superficial; it is as much the expression of an exuberant collective imagination as are the novels of Carlos Fuentes or the murals of Diego Rivera. It is an imagination that connects and assembles. Mexicans conspire to blur the lines between the genres of everyday life, elevating a silver-masked wrestler to the status first of film star, then of street savior (providing much resonance for that dazzling bricoleur, the Zapatista Subcomandante Marcos). Or, with a few deft gestures, they may arrange food, photos, candles, and more mysterious elements into shrines or yet more elusive still-lifes, vaguely religious and softly pulsating with life.

Discovering and representing these dimensions of local life requires time—a patient conversation with the people and the place. But can the photographer, the camera, converse? It is now fashionable to note the lack of transparency of the lens. Behind the camera, we are told, are the intention, focus, prejudice, and agenda of the photographer. Is there not a chance that in so stressing the "determined" character of the photo we are underestimating the possibility that the subject or object of "focus" can emerge or even assert him-, her-, or itself in the space of the photo? If the photograph is not a transparent representation of the world "out there," neither is it simply a projection of the artist, an opaque overlay. If the photographer has a strong eye but a light hand and leaves open, as Maeve Hickey does, a conversational space that allows the surprise, wonder, and uncertainty of both mediator and audience to be left intact, then the subjects can look back through the lens. We recognize them in their enigmatic smiles, mysterious shrines, joyous leaps, or mouths set in bitter resolve as they thread their way through the maze.

The disrupted and disorienting world of Nogales is, ironically but not illogically, a dynamic and creative one. This photographer is clearly drawn to the resulting rich range of aesthetic expression in all forms, including visual images. To photograph in Mexico is to practice that art in a world where people understand the power and magic of the image, where they know that any image can become more than simply a representation. In the right place, the image becomes the thing itself. Religious pictures such as the Virgin of Guadalupe come to mind, of course, but the mundane family photo can rise to the same plane of power when placed in a shrine in order to direct the healing force of some saint to the people in the photo. Not that creativity or expressiveness is found only in the religious sphere. In fact, the

volatile tension and blurring from one realm to the other is irresistible to the artist's eye. Just when you think that the Virgin of Guadalupe dangling from the taxi driver's mirror might as well be a pair of fuzzy dice, he clutches the plastic statue to his heart and tearfully calls on "mi patronita!"

As sculptor as well as photographer, Maeve Hickey is clearly attuned to this tension in the creative act, and not only in her own work but in the movement of the matador, the song and costume of the mariachi, and even the flashed gang sign of the tunnel kid. Equally, she finds it in the object created: the rock painting of an angel's head, the Paul Bond cowboy boots, or the mission ruin. Taken together, her photographs do not depict simply a brute world of death, drugs, and state repression. Neither do they conjure a hidden, gentle, beautiful Mexico. Rather, they explore the dynamic confrontation of both these realities and the inner tensions that animate them.

The writer follows the artist's lead, wandering the streets and entering into conversations meant to explore and reveal, rather than explain. The people he meets lead him as well to see beyond the simple if striking dichotomies. For if the border is a place of stark contrasts or of hidden folk and local life, it is also one of contradiction, surprise, and mystery. The border attracts and repels, links and divides, and therein perhaps lies its central contradiction, a contradiction that produces endless ironies. Most ironic, perhaps, is the fact that in this dynamic and fragile world, the illusion of cultural stability, of a coherent identity over time and space, can be especially crucial to survival—of the individual, of the group, and even of the state.

Maintaining such illusions requires creativity and performance. Identity—whether individual or collective—is a striking example, for it needs endless reenactment. For those on the U.S. side of Nogales, the vast majority of whom are Mexican Americans, identity varies greatly, and its performance is a complex and typically inconsistent matter. Those who still have one foot planted on either side of the line—*fronterizos* like Claudia—may be untroubled by the ambiguity of their "position." They are rooted in locality, and rather than feeling betwixt and between two nations, they are more likely to be at home precisely where they are, in a thoroughly coherent and familiar human landscape that happens to have a border running through it. But for many others in Nogales, Arizona, and farther north, the links have been or are weakening, and their identity can require a more public and certainly self-conscious performance of Mexican-ness, in the form of mariachi singing, mural painting, and so on.

South of the border, things are different. There, too, are the old *fronterizos*—but they are likely to feel less comfortable in a town bursting at the seams. Those who can afford to, retreat to cool interiors, walling themselves in against the sea of poor streaming in around them. As for those displaced newcomers, they try, like all immigrants, to create little islands of old kin and neighbors. But given the flux and shortage of housing, they rarely achieve more than a tiny cluster; in the colonias of Nogales there are no "Guadalajaran" neighborhoods. It is instead a world of high mobility, danger, flux, opportunity, disorder, and disaster. In these circumstances, visible signs and symbols of Mexican culture—strolling musicians, bullfights—may find their dramatic space, but new cultural forms also arise. Amulets, for example, now feature portraits of Jesús Malverde, and border balladeers sing *narcocorridos*—in both cases, the exploits of the latest outlaws are shaped by and for the folk/popular genres of border adventure and resistance. Or the gang signs and cholo dress of the Barrio Libre gang—the tunnel kids: crucial gestures in their search for physical and cultural shelter.

Finally, even for the nation-states of Mexico and the U.S., the contingency of the border calls for the performance of its alleged cultural and political reality—the prevailing flux demands the illusion of consistency. Like all borders, it is meant to eliminate any such ambiguity by making utterly clear, utterly concrete, where one nation—in every possible sense of the word—stops and another begins. Thus, a border, especially a border like this one, seems the very embodiment of state power.

Yet in another sense the existence of the border demonstrates the contingency of the state. For if borders can be taken for granted by secure states, this one clearly is not. Rather, it is constantly "performed." Indeed, both sides are so heavily patrolled by armed personnel that they seem to be occupied territories—and so they are, if by their own governments. But the play needs a larger cast and audience, for the border is there only if everyone acts as if it were. Such a drama requires an elaborate set: fences, walls, guard boxes, uniformed personnel, and of course the literally ubiquitous green cruisers—*los chiles verdes*—of the Border Patrol, all of which remind the players/audience that they have entered the theater of the state.

But the more theatrical all this border activity becomes, the more ephemeral it may seem. Why are they trying so hard? All the walls, fences, police, and so on might as easily represent the state's failure to contain or stem the virtual tidal wave of desire that threatens at every moment and at every point to breach and subvert all barriers.

The dramas of life on the border are not only brutal but also subtle, ambiguous, sometimes fleeting, and often contradictory. Here, the photographer and writer offer images that do not resolve these contradictions and ironies, whether in personal identity or the power of the state, but rather preserve them by highlighting and foregrounding that which doesn't fit the frame. In those images there can be awful power and danger, but also, we hope, a sense of the exuberance and mystery of *ambos Nogales*.

■ PHOTOGRAPHS